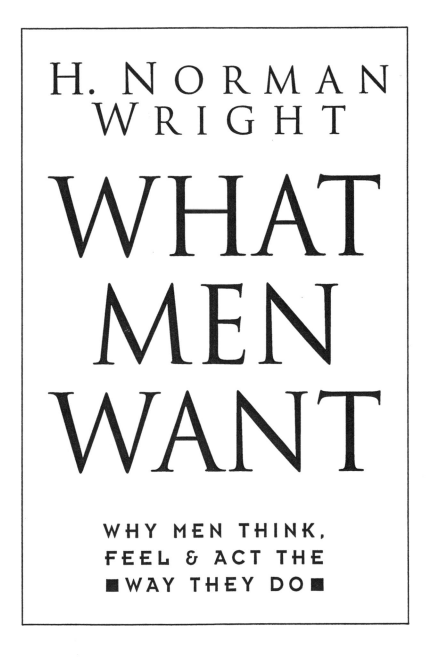

H. NORMAN WRIGHT

WHAT MEN WANT

WHY MEN THINK, FEEL & ACT THE ■WAY THEY DO■

H. NORMAN WRIGHT

WHAT MEN WANT

WHY MEN THINK, FEEL & ACT THE ■WAY THEY DO■

Regal Books
A Division of Gospel Light
Ventura, California, U.S.A.

Regal Books
A Division of Gospel Light
Ventura, California, U.S.A.
Printed in U.S.A.

Regal Books is a ministry of Gospel Light, an evangelical Christian publisher dedicated to serving the local church. We believe God's vision for Gospel Light is to provide church leaders with biblical, user-friendly materials that will help them evangelize, disciple and minister to children, youth and families.

It is our prayer that this Regal book will help you discover biblical truth for your own life and help you meet the needs of others. May God richly bless you.

For a free catalog of resources from Regal Books/Gospel Light please contact your Christian supplier or call 1-800-4-GOSPEL.

Library of Congress Cataloging-in-Publication Data
Wright, H. Norman.
    What men want / H. Norman Wright.
        p. c.m.
    Includes bibliographical references.
    ISBN 0-8307-1593-2 (hardcover)
    1. Men. 2. Man-woman relationships. I. Title.
HQ1090.W77 1996   96-11399
305.3—dc20   CIP

1 2 3 4 5 6 7 8 9 10 11 12 13 14 / 02 01 00 99 98 97 96

Rights for publishing this book in other languages are contracted by Gospel Literature International (GLINT). GLINT also provides technical help for the adaptation, translation and publishing of Bible study resources and books in scores of languages worldwide. For further information, contact GLINT, P.O. Box 4060, Ontario, CA 91761-1003, U.S.A., or the publisher.

CONTENTS

Is What
They Say
About Men
True?

Men. That's the word. The reason for this book.

This is not the first book about the subject, nor will it be the last; but it may be different. Your response to it might be different. Every reader's response might be different.

It is not written to fulfill preconceived beliefs or answer everyone's questions. You may at times think it is light, and at other times heavy and sobering. It may raise more questions than it answers. It may reveal something you never knew, or it may confirm what you already knew or suspected, prompting you to reason "I was right all along." It may anger you, causing you to think that what is said is an unfair conspiracy against men. Or you may feel they get a fair shake.

Ultimately, this book's purpose is to reveal—to disclose—the private lives of men. It is designed to encourage you to think, to react and then to do something about what you've read.

No lack of opinions exist today about men. Talk shows,

tabloid articles, serious journal articles, videos and scores of books all have basically one purpose—to help us understand what makes men tick and how to respond to them.

WHAT DO YOU
BELIEVE ABOUT MEN?

The following statements are typical of what we read and hear about men today. How do you respond to these statements? Are they just opinions and stereotypes, or are they true facts about most men?

- Culture plays a greater part in determining male-female differences than does biology.
- Men need to think about feelings before they can talk about them whereas women can feel, think and talk simultaneously.
- A man's "on" button for sex is never off.
- Men are more visually oriented than women are.
- Women have different emotions than men have.
- The brain structure of a man is different from that of a woman.
- Men don't like to talk about issues late at night when they are tired because they feel less in control and fear that the discussion will go on and on.
- Because most men are goal oriented, they get frustrated if they can't complete the thought they are sharing.
- Most men do not want to talk either during sex or while completing a task around the house because interruptions distract them.
- Men hesitate to read self-help and marriage books or go for counseling because they don't want to admit failure.
- Men are geared to give at work, but to receive at home.
- Men forget their problems by not talking about them, whereas women rid themselves of problems by remembering and discussing them.

- Men need appreciation to feel nurtured.
- Men try to put their feelings into actions rather than words because "doing" provides greater relief than "discussing" does for them.
- Men don't offer solutions to women to shut them up. They just want to solve the issues women share with them.
- When a man is pressured by a woman to give more, he pulls away; but when a man is not expected to give more, he wants to.
- Most men have tunnel vision because they don't use their brains holistically.
- It is difficult for men to concentrate on issues at home if they have too much stress and hassle at work.
- When a man hears the phrase "You don't understand," instead of becoming more open to new information, he closes up even more.
- Because of his brain structure, it is difficult for a man to think straight and share when he is experiencing strong feelings.
- Men don't like to be wrong, suspect they are wrong or have women know they are wrong before they themselves know they are wrong.
- Men consider requests for more information, reasons for what they are doing or clarification as either personal challenges or accusations that they are wrong.
- Men are not as verbally skilled as women because they differ from women in early brain development.
- Men naturally like structure and discussion about numbers and statistics. That's just the way they are.
- Men are concerned with themselves first—then others.
- Men value control. That is why they avoid the disclosures necessary for developing intimacy. They perceive intimacy as a threat to control.
- Men respond to loss and grieve differently than women do.

- Men are more immediately decisive than women are.
- The fear of being wrong is a driving force for men.
- Men are more apt to avoid conflict with women than women are with men.

Well, what do you think? Are these true, partially true or not at all true? What, if anything, can be done to improve the misunderstandings between men and women?

We could guess endlessly about men, and speculate forever about these questions. In this book, however, I've chosen to draw from what men have said about themselves. Much of what you will read emanates from my own counseling, from a questionnaire I sent to 700 other counselors and from a survey of men themselves. I think you'll find what men say about themselves especially helpful.

If you are interested in a word from men, about men, read on.

REFLECTING ON THIS CHAPTER

1. Which of the previous statements commonly heard about men do you believe to be true? Which are false stereotypes?
2. As a man, which of these traits create problems in your own life and/or relationships?
3. As a woman, which of these traits create problems in your relationship with your partner?
4. Do you think current articles and books have overdone what some have called "male bashing"?
5. What is the difference between this practice and healthy discussions about how men can grow personally and develop healthier relationships with women?

THE DIALOGUE

"And then there was man...human...male. How did he become what he is? Who conceived the idea of creating him as he is? I wonder who...."

"I did."

"Who's that?"

"It is I."

"But who are...?"

"God."

"God?"

"Yes, God. I made man. Do you have some questions about men?"

"Well, yes, but I didn't expect to hear from...or talk with...."

"God?"

"Well, yes now that You mention it."

"Why wouldn't you expect to hear from Me? After all, it was my idea."

"I just didn't think...well. You must have been listening in."

"I always listen. I hear everything. That's who I am."

(Silence.)

"Do you want to know why men act the way they do?"

"Sure. So do a lot of other people, especially women."

"Well, let's look at the beginning. That is, the beginning as you think about it. There was no beginning of time for Me. I have always been and always will be.

"At the beginning of time there was no universe or earth as you know it. I created the earth and My Spirit moved over the surface of the waters. I created the light and said *it was good*. I created the heavens, the waters, and the dry land and *they were good*. For the first time there was form. There were shapes. I also created the earth to bring forth vegetation—trees, plants, fruit—and *it too was good*. I made the lights in the heavens to govern the day and the night and, oh, *it was good!*"

"I wish I had been there. I get excited just hearing You describe it. Once I was in a cave deep in the bowels of the earth. It was the darkest dark I've ever experienced. And then...then someone flipped a switch and massive lights came on. Our eyes were flooded with so much light that it reminded me of pictures I had seen reflecting the burst of an atomic blast. Was it anything like that in the beginning?"

"Yes, like that and more. But what I had created was merely the foundation for what was to come. Later—the fifth day—I created the living things: the creatures and animals and birds in the sea and on the earth. As the birds flew, the fish and other creatures swam, the animals walked and crawled. *It was good.* If only you could have witnessed the astonishment on the faces of those first creations as they saw their kind and all those who were different!

"And then...I created *man*. In My image I created him. I formed him out of the dust of the ground and breathed into his nostrils the breath of life. He was just a little lower than the angels. He was special. He was more complex than any of the other creatures. He not only had a body, but also a soul. Most important, he was created in *My image*. He was created as a rational, social and spiritual being. He was created to be My representative on earth.

"All of My creation was good—*it was very good*. I was delighted with My work. I approved of it. I took pleasure in it. I rejoiced over My creation of mankind, male and female. I rejoiced then as I do now in doing good for them, as a bridegroom rejoices over a bride. The difference is that the honeymoon never ends with Me. I rejoice over My creation with all My heart.

"Not only do I rejoice over them with loud singing, but the

angels also joyfully sing over mankind; and when they do, it is I who leads the singing. I love what I have created. They are never out of My thoughts.

"Do My descriptions convey to you the importance of My work?"

"Oh, yes, I get the point. It sounds very special."

"Did you know there was an audience present when I created all that I just described for you?"

"No, I didn't."

"There was. I recorded my conversation with Job in Scripture. Read Job 38. I asked him, 'Where were you when I laid the foundation of the earth when the morning stars sang together and all the sons of God [angels] shouted for joy?' The angels watched. Can you imagine the awe and wonder they experienced when they saw what had never been seen before?"

"I guess the movie renditions I've seen of the Creation were nothing compared to what really happened."

"You're right. There's never been anything as spectacular as the beginning. But I've jumped a bit ahead in the story, so I will regress to the time when I created man. Only one thing was *not good*: man was alone.

"So I created woman. My image is reflected in both male and female. Neither is inferior or superior to the other. I created them with many similarities. They have many common emotions, needs and attributes. They're also different in many ways. I created them with the capacity for intimate relationships, to know Me and other humans. They have a need for each other. It is a good need, because each one is incomplete without the other. I created them to complement each other, but never to lose their separateness or identities. This was and is My design.

"Their humility is evidenced in their need for each other. Each of them is a completion of the other and is dependent upon the other. Each fills up the empty places of the other. When a man and a woman come together for life they are to leave their parents—leave, not linger. The relationship with their parents is to be severed and abandoned, in a healthy way. They are to cleave to each other, to adhere in a unique oneness in all areas of life."

"So You purposely made them as different as they are?"

"Yes, I did. You're suggesting it was accidental?"

"Oh, no...no, not at all. But, sometimes...."

"Many have wondered. You're not the first. In addition to the obvious physical differences, many other differences are also evident in their responses and behaviors."

"So what happened?"

"What happened when? Where?"

"I mean, what happened to men?...and to women for that matter? What went wrong? It seems from what You have said that they were created as a perfect match. The way You've described it, they were meant to be allies—but so often men and women relate as adversaries.

"And we've got all these problems of divorce, unfaithfulness, abuse, blame, suspicion and harassment. It wasn't supposed to be this way. Why did something You created get so messed up?"

"Sin."

"Sin?"

"Yes, sin 'messed it up,' as you put it!"

"Well, couldn't You have prevented that?"

"Yes, but I chose to create man as a free being with a will and the ability to choose between good and evil—to choose to love and worship Me."

"But something went wrong!"

"You know the story. Satan clothed in the form of a serpent came to them and spoke to Eve. He convinced her to disobey Me. She invited Adam to join her, and instead of saying, 'No, we need to obey God' he caved in. This was the first sign of passivity. The man-woman relationship and everything else became disordered.

"I went to them for our time of fellowship. I knew where they were and what they had done, just as I know about everyone today. You can't be omnipresent and omniscient and not know, can you?"

"No, I guess not."

"Adam and Eve now knew shame and fear, so they hid from Me. From that moment until now, men have continued to refine this tendency to hide, not just from Me, but also from intimacy with the women in their lives. Adam hid.

"He then began to blame. First he blamed his wife, and then he blamed Me for giving her to him. Ever since Adam's time, men have tended to be defensive. They often interpret innocent questions as accusations. And the blame that started in the Garden...oh, men have cultivated that ability well! The role I assigned to Adam has been distorted."

"Ah, wait a minute. Men are defensive by nature? I don't think we're so defensive."

(Silence.)

"Well, perhaps some men are...but we do get accused a lot...."

(Silence.)

"All right, we're defensive. Please continue, or is that it?"

"There's much more. In the Garden, both Adam and Eve could relate emotionally. They were able to give one another the gift of understanding. Not now. Now, if a woman wants understanding from a man, what does she get?"

"Solutions, answers, advice...."

"Usually it's advice, because giving advice is easier and safer than relating emotionally. Instead, it generates further distance in a relationship. It's safer for a man to give solutions than to empathize.

"The question I asked Adam in the Garden is the question I continue to ask men (and so do women): *'Where are you?'*

"There were many consequences from the Fall. When Satan, that murderer and falsifier, induced the Fall of My children, the results were devastating. Humans became liable to physical death, eternal punishment and spiritual death. They were alienated from fellowship with Me. If they had not sinned, they could have continued living in the Garden.

"A relationship that was meant to be complementary became competitive. Eve's desire was to control Adam. What I created to be a perfect balance resulted in a deteriorating imbalance and a clash of wills. The mutual security and love they shared in each other's presence was first tarnished, then it was broken.

"The result has been a power struggle. Man's strength became perverted; and his perverted sense of strength led to domination rather than loving leadership in marriage. Actually, not just in marriage, but in all male-female relationships. The sexual and emotional exploitation of women is a result. This tragedy is manifested by thwarting the giftedness of many women.

"Shame about their physical and emotional nakedness also entered into their relationship."

"Whoa—what do You mean by *emotional* nakedness? *Physical* I understand, but...."

"Don't you see? Adam and Eve no longer fully trusted each other. They could no longer love each other perfectly. They became suspicious of each other. Intimate sharing was now filtered through cautious restraint. The transparent love that once flowed naturally was now an effort.

"Humans learned to live with reserve, hesitation and a bent toward self-protection. Freely given love between men and women was substituted with demands.

"Although both were created for closeness and connectedness, they began to pursue independence. Independence is another distortion resulting from the Fall. Men view a lack of independence as synonymous with incompetence and insecurity.

"This imperfect love between men and women is demonstrated in an imperfect love toward their children. When these children consider marriage, they bring their hopes and expectations for redeeming the imperfect love of their parents to the marriage. As these redemptive desires and expectations go unfulfilled, they turn into demands."

"Well, the more I hear, the more I wonder why You created people with the power to choose. Wouldn't it have been better just to sort of, well...*make* them obedient to begin with? You know—build obedience into them in a gene or something?"

"Can you really share love and fellowship with those who have no choice in how they respond? Would you honestly feel desired, cared for and valued, unless the other person had the opportunity to choose?"

"No, but the ability to choose sure upset everything, didn't it?"

"Yes, it did. And it still does. But there's more.

"I created men and women with a full range of emotions, as I said earlier. Each emotion was necessary and designed for a purpose. Original sin, however, seeped into and polluted their emotional lives.

"Men initially needed anger for energy and protection; but now, they often use it to hurt others and defend themselves. If only they could see that anger never draws people closer. Instead, it widens the gulf between them.

"Men need to control, win, save face, prove themselves and avoid admitting weakness. I did not create men with a fear of intimacy or being loved. This fear is a distortion from the Fall.

"Fear was originally an emotion that was beneficial to humans. It was never intended to be included in the man-woman relationship. Once trust was broken, doubts entered and unhealthy fear took root. Humans began to doubt My love for them as well as their love for each other. The greater the level of fear, the less love is experienced.

"Fear is a destructive force in relationships between men and women. When men or women live in fear of each other, fear perpetuates the distance between them.

"The damage from sin was extensive. Adam and Eve's minds had the potential to be wonderfully creative. But sin contaminated their minds. Their difficulties originate in the distortions of their thinking. You'll remember reading a passage I recorded in Genesis 6:5 that explains how I 'saw that the wickedness of man was great in the earth, and that every imagination and intention of all human thinking was only evil continually.'

"Remember?"

"Oh yes, I remember reading it. I always wondered why so many passages pertain to controlling or refocusing our thought lives. As I read Scripture, I notice that fear was a dominating factor throughout history."

"It was. It still is. It will always be a struggle. Just look at the history of the world and you see the results from the misuse of one of the greatest gifts I ever gave to humans: their minds, their imaginations. Their tendencies to see others and themselves negatively, to become overly competitive, overly focused and task oriented to a fault are all perversions of the mind-set I gave to them.

"This is especially true in the area of sexuality. An interesting maxim exists today about the difference between the sexual expressions of men and women. It says that men give affection to get sex, and women give sex to get affection. That was not at all the way I intended it to be.

"Sin's effects have negatively influenced both men and women in society. The sexuality of women has been squelched and men have been encouraged to downplay the importance of their needs for intimacy and expression of emotions. Sex has become the consuming drive and interest for some men, totally obscuring its original purpose and intent. But I don't need to tell you that, do I?"

"No. I'm the one who raised the question. It wasn't an academic question, either. I'd like to better understand what makes me and other men tick. Sometimes I feel like Paul when he said in the seventh chapter of Romans 'the things I want to do I don't do and the things I don't want to do I do,' or something like that.

"It would be helpful if men and women understood each other more. Perhaps it would be possible for us to move back to Your original design and become complementary allies. Deep down maybe that's what we all want.

"But I guess most of us don't always want to pay the price of growing, stretching and changing. It means admitting I'm not complete the way I am...I could improve. It means considering the requests of others and acknowledging they may be right after all. Satan and sin really did a number on us."

"Yes, he did. Because of the damage caused by sin, people went their own way, not experiencing their full potential and not having a perfect man to look to as an example.

"But that changed when I invaded the floundering history of humanity with a child named Jesus. He was a complete man in His humanity, tempted in every way as every other human being—but He did not sin.

"He was very masculine. He fulfilled His messianic journey as a warrior against wrong for those who needed Him. He felt, He hurt, He was wounded. He suffered and was tempted in all things that He might identify with all people. No matter what anyone struggles with today, that person is not alone. Jesus can identify. When anyone, man or woman, puts his or her life into the hands of Jesus, that which was lost is now found and being restored. Humans can once again experience a relationship with Me. And after all, isn't that what life is all about?"

"Perhaps sin keeps men and women from responding to that offer."

"You are beginning to understand. And it all comes down to one thing, doesn't it?"

"What's that?"

"You've forgotten so soon."

"Oh...not really. I'm just not sure."

"A choice. You have to decide what you will do, and then do it."

"That sounds familiar. Someone else was faced with a choice, wasn't he?"

"Yes, he was. But Adam didn't make the best choice."

"Well, I'll have to think some more. I hope I make a wise choice."

"For your sake, for women's sake, for humanity's sake, for My sake—I hope you do, too."

REFLECTING ON THIS CHAPTER

1. Why is it important for men to understand the biblical truth that God called creation "very good"?

2. The author says that men were created to be "God's representatives on earth." What *privileges* and *obligations* are implied by this truth?

3. How were the emotions of *fear* and *anger* beneficial to primitive man? How can they become destructive today?

4. What forces in a marriage can turn men and women from *allies*, as God intended, into *adversaries*?

5. Evaluate the common observation that "men give affection to get sex, and women give sex to get affection."

THE PRIVATE
MALE

"I like privacy. I like knowing certain thoughts and issues I'm dealing with are known by no one else. There is satisfaction in handling the stuff of life by myself and resolving it. It's a good feeling. It's comfortable—reassuring.

"Others tell me I need to talk about it, to share my inner self with people, especially my wife. But why? What's in it for me? What good will sharing my feelings accomplish? I think I can handle what's going on, but I wonder if anyone else can. My wife might not understand. She might be threatened by what I share...or want to resolve it with me.

"So then we talk about it for some time. It's not private anymore. It's not mine anymore. It's like someone let down the drawbridge to my castle and invaders disrupted everything. I'd rather control the drawbridge myself. And if I need help or assistance, then I'll ask for it. I think...."

Sound familiar? It's a monologue that could be voiced by any number of men.

Who can understand the inner workings of a man's mind? Oh, that we could x-ray the thought processes of the adult male. I am one of them—a man around age 60. That is not an easy admission, either to say or to write. It has a sense of finality to it, like going into the fourth quarter of the football game of life.

When a man turns 50, he is thinking about changes. The clock is ticking and he no longer thinks *if* I die, but *when* I die. He no longer thinks about what he can accomplish and achieve, but what he can do with the time he has left before he dies.

I feel that way. Most other men approaching the sixtieth year of their lives do, too. I continually ask myself, "What do I want to do and enjoy in the years remaining, and how can I be used for God's kingdom in these years?"

Almost 10 years before writing this book, I wrote my first book about men. I was younger then, and this is what I said about where I was in life:

> Joyce and I will turn 50 in 1987. I tended to ignore my 40th birthday, but I have considered more and more how to celebrate this next milestone in a special way. Why? Perhaps it's a way of accepting, facing, and welcoming the half-century mark. This also involves recognizing all that God has done for me during times of delight, enjoyment, fun, unique experiences, pain, sorrow, and loss. It is a time of thanking Him for bringing a fullness and meaning to life no matter what has occurred. It is also a way of saying I am ready for whatever He has in the future—and it is all right not to know what to expect. That's risky. The unknown and unpredictable become the known and predictable because of who is in charge of my life and life itself.[1]

I had forgotten I'd written that. But I believed it then, and I continue to believe it for the upcoming 10 years.

I wrote in those days about the unknown and unpredictable. Little did I know then that one of those unforeseen events would be the death of my 22-year-old retarded son. As parents, we never expect to outlive our children, but it does happen. Matthew's entrance into my life changed me, so did his departure. I talk about it freely. I have to. I need to. Most men don't talk about such experiences, except within their own minds.

It is easier for us to talk to ourselves because there is no risk involved that way. We like our privacy; but privacy carries a high price tag and one of its costly premiums is silence. Silence shouts loudly in relationships. It can be deafening. It conveys a plurality of messages. It is fraught with potential for great misunderstanding.

Silence leaves in its wake responses that range from wonderment to confusion. Silence frustrates. It raises concern, generates doubts, distances people from one another and does very little to create positive relationships. Silence compels us to ask questions.

Men ask, "Is it me? Am I the only one to feel or think this way? Am I odd or normal? Does anyone else struggle with this? Why can't I be different? Must I change? Is it possible to change? Am I OK as I am? Why do I feel as if something is missing inside of me? What would others think if I revealed this to them? Would I be accepted or rejected? What if I don't know what to do? What if I do the right thing, or the wrong thing?"

In his book *The Seven Seasons of a Man's Life*, Patrick Morley takes this questioning even further:

> Men today are filled with anger, fears, worries, and doubts. They are under a great deal of stress. It often takes two incomes just to keep up. The half-life of a college education is about four years. Every other marriage ends in divorce.
>
> The world's answers have not worked. Men find themselves feeling empty inside, like there is something missing. They are lonely and wonder, *What is the meaning of it all?* Men feel guilty about their pasts and are afraid of their futures. Men today want something satisfying. Even in the church, *especially* in the church, men are hungry for God. A pervasive feeling is that "there must be more— there's gotta be." Men are coming to the end of themselves. They are reaching out for answers.[2]

Men are full of questions. Whom do they ask? All too often they ask themselves. They raise the issues and then look to themselves for the answers. But how can the inquirer be the expert? A mental conversation may be safe, but it is limited in its resources.

Women also ask questions about men. "Why is he like that? What's going on inside of him? I'd give anything to know. Is there anything going on inside of him? Why does he shut me out so much? What does he think about? What is he afraid of sharing, and why? Is he afraid of me? I'm not going to bite!"

Men are asking, "Why don't I speak up and share what's really going on inside me?"

Women are asking, "Why doesn't he speak up and share what is going on inside of him?"

The issue of silence in men is as old as the beginning of time. Larry Crabb discusses the subject in the early pages of his recent book, *The Silence of Adam.*

Where was Adam when the serpent tempted Eve? The Bible says that after Eve was deceived by Satan, she took some of the forbidden fruit "...and ate it. She also gave some to her husband, *who was with her* (emphasis added), and he ate it" (Genesis 3:6).

Was Adam there the whole time? Was he standing right next to his wife while the serpent tricked her with his cunning? Was he there, listening to every word?

If he was—and there is good reason to think so— then a big question must be asked: *WHY DIDN'T HE SAY ANYTHING?*

Since Adam every man has had a natural inclination to remain silent when he should speak. A man is most comfortable in situations in which he knows exactly what to do. When things get confusing and scary, his insides tighten and he backs away.[3]

If you are a man, is silence a part of your life? Do you view silence as an enemy or a friend, a hinderer who suffocates your words or an advocate who speaks for you?

If you are a woman, is there silence in your relationship? These are questions to ask, consider and hopefully to answer.

Men today are addressing the issues and concerns about their inner questions. They are getting tired of the elevator lifestyle. I will explain.

Whether 2 or 12 passengers stand in the cramped space of an elevator, nobody talks. People enter the elevator as strangers, and they depart as strangers. They are careful not to touch each other with their bodies or even their words. No one looks at anyone else. Eye contact is avoided and everyone glares at the number board as though they might miss their floors! Where are the signs that prohibit them from looking, touching or talking? A silent conspiracy persists and everyone participates in it. Isolation is the plan.

Nothing is worse than isolation. Life is incomplete when it is lived alone and unshared. Isolation is counterproductive to God's creative plan. He said, "It is not good for the man to be alone" (Gen. 2:18). Interesting, that was the first time God called something "not good."

A graphic illustration of isolation emanates from the pen of Max Lucado. He was walking through a graveyard in San Antonio when he came upon a marker. This is what he says:

> Then I saw it. It was chiseled into a tombstone on the northern end of the cemetery. The stone marks the destination of the body of Grace Llewellen Smith. No date of birth is listed, no date of death. Just the names of her two husbands, and this epitaph:
>
> "Sleeps, but rests not.
> Loves, but was loved not.
> Tried to please, but pleased not.
> Died as she lived—alone."
>
> Words of futility.
> I stared at the marker and wondered about Grace Llewellen Smith. I wondered about her life. I wondered if she'd written the words...or just

lived them. I wondered if she deserved the pain. I wondered if she was bitter or beaten. I wondered if she was plain. I wondered if she was beautiful. I wondered why some lives are so fruitful while others are so futile.

I caught myself wondering aloud, "Mrs. Smith, what broke your heart?"[4]

Thousands of Grace Smiths exist today—both men and women. Some people live as though they have been immunized against close, intimate relationships.

Isolation is a potent killer. It destroys not only the person who isolates, but also the relationship. It is time to stop the elevator and say, "Here I am. This is who I am. I am somebody. I have questions and I want answers. I am going to reveal who I am and really live." It is time to get out of the elevator.

For years, men have learned to pretend. We were taught to say, "Everything is OK. I can handle it. I know what I'm doing. My life is together." But for many men life isn't OK, and we don't think we can handle it. One of the popular songs when I was in high school was titled "The Great Pretender." How many times have I and others I have talked to felt that was our theme song?

Whether Christian men or not, we all pretend. We say, "I've got it under control," but the real voice inside cries, "I'm anxious, scared and worried that I won't make it. Will someone pray for me? Will someone help me? Please help me find out what's missing inside."

THE PLIGHT OF MEN

Look at the books written about men by men. The indictments against men have come as much from themselves as from women. Either the indictments are accurate or no one is bothering to counter them. Listen to what has been said since the beginning of the '90s.

Vern Becker, in his book *The Real Man Inside,* talks about himself and his friends, all of whom had wives who left them. At first they had blamed their wives for being the ones to walk out.

We helped with the kids or with household chores, but usually we had to be asked. Our friendships, our church involvement, even our family activities seemed to be carried on out of obligation rather than conviction. Our faith survived mostly in terms of beliefs that we assented to, but we felt little or no personal connection with God. We also felt somewhat confused about what our roles were. Though most of us pursued careers, none of us had a clear sense of what we wanted out of life, and few of us did much to find out. There was a kind of monotony to life, at least to our inner life.

In short, we lived empty, passive lives. We had little sense of our identity as men. We could be nice, we could be helpful, we could even be sensitive; but we didn't know how to be real, how to seize the day and live out of our deepest desire. So how could we offer much of ourselves to our wives?[5]

Many men have identified with the following story of one man's search. If you're a man, is this you? If you're a woman, does this revelation surprise you?

For much of my life, I've felt that empty place inside. Something was missing in me. It was as if I were built on some cosmic assembly line, and someone forgot to put in a critical part. I have looked diligently to find it. I've searched for it in seminars, listening carefully for the word or phrase that would make me complete. I've studied book after book, hoping for some gem of wisdom to leap from the page. I've used passionate, talented friends, attempting to get something from them that I thought I didn't have, hoping to absorb into myself whatever they could give. But my search has been futile. The missing part has remained a mystery.

As I've spoken with other men about my

search, most recognize my quest as their own. "I know what you're talking about," they say, with a hint of relief in their voices. "I thought I was the only one." Though their stories are different, they each talk eloquently about something that is missing inside them. The search for the missing piece is varied, and what they find to fill themselves works only for a time. Eventually it fails.

My story reflects a reality that is present in every man. There is something inside all of us that yearns to be expressed. It is both passionate and creative. It doesn't need to be learned. It doesn't need to be created; it already has been. It is there, built into men at birth, waiting for release. And when it is released, it is terrifying. I know that now, but for many years I did not.[6]

28

It is difficult to go through life or complete anything when a piece of the puzzle is missing. What can we do?

First, we must acknowledge that a piece is missing, that an empty place actually exists. Then we must let others share the secret so they can help us with our search for the missing piece. Men were not created to live, work, love or die in isolation.

Doctors provide us with both a diagnosis and a prognosis for our symptoms. They tell us what the problem is and then what the probable outcome will be. Often the problem can only be corrected with exploratory corrective surgery—major surgery. Think of this chapter as exploratory corrective surgery. Once the incision has been made, we must expand our search to identify some of the other major issues about the private lives of men.

QUESTIONS AND ANSWERS— WITH DIFFICULTY

I asked men throughout the country to disclose the thoughts and subjects they hesitate to share with their wives. I was amazed. It was like pulling teeth to get men to respond to a simple questionnaire of four questions! Their hesitancy, resistance and brevity of answers confirmed the extent of the male privacy problem. Yet scores of men did contribute significant information.

In response to the question *What subject(s) do you think men hesitate most in bringing up or discussing with women?*—one attorney gave a summation of his experience with men.

> Being able to nudge men into expressing the subjects they most hesitate to bring up or discuss with women is an almost impossible chore. It is tantamount to a confession that men find hard to share. I am an attorney who is a certified legal specialist in family law, and in the 20 years I have been practicing, I have interviewed thousands of men who were experiencing marital problems trying to ascertain what were their chief concerns. If I was lucky, I could barely get the men to identify *one* subject they hesitated most in discussing with women. Generating conversation was next to impossible, although it was clear that many subjects were of concern. The biggest problem, I think, is simply getting men to discuss any issues at all with women. Certainly some subjects men are less hesitant to bring up or discuss with women than others. I think these include finances, family budget, social activities, sports and to a lesser extent, personal intimacy. If there is one category to define all the subjects that men hesitate to talk about, it would be in the area of emotions. Men do not like to discuss their hurts, stress, lack of accomplishment and questions of their energy. All of these, of course, would fall under the general heading of inability to express personal feelings.

This is how several other men addressed the question:

> *Anything personal.* Particularly anything personal about themselves. I don't think most men get into much "self-examination." It's tough enough

29

to answer questions about how you feel, but it gets much tougher when my wife responds with "Why do you feel this way?"

Our insecurities, weaknesses, fears, vulnerability. So much of our identity (personally and culturally) centers on being strong, on being "the protector." Sometimes we feel as though we can't or shouldn't show our vulnerabilities without compromising our masculine identity, which is, of course, not so (knowing it's not so is one thing, but feeling that it's not so is tough).

Emotional intimacy. It is very hard for me to explain to my wife how I feel about things and situations that affect me deeply. I don't seem to have the right words to say. And even if I could express myself, I would become very vulnerable in front of her. I need to be the man in the house, and men don't cry in front of their wives.

Fears and *insecurities* and *the sense of inadequacy* I often experience. Another subject that's difficult to discuss is my *struggle with lust,* though I think my difficulty in discussing it is also rooted in fear: fear of rejection, fear of hurting her, fear of facing my own corruption.

FEAR AND THE NEED TO CONTROL

It is sad to hear how much of our lives as men is dominated by fear. Ironically, we choose to be controlled by it when what we really want is to be in control of everything in our lives! Men's emotional withdrawal costs big time.

Robert Hicks said it well: "We can hide in the closets of competition, use emotional walls to protect us or flee from the reality of our deepest fears, but when we do, we flee from our own manhood."[7]

Although men camouflage their fears, the telltale evidence of fear surfaces in many ways. Rigidity and explosiveness can be traced to fear, as can obsessive quests and unattainable pursuits.

Excessive competitiveness and *personal dumping on themselves* for underachievement are reflections of other fears—of losing, failing or being second best.

Men fear being powerless, and will go to extremes to be in control and avoid situations in which they feel out of control. As a result, men are typically seen behind the wheel of a car rather than in the passenger seat, especially if their wives are with them. They seldom admit, "I think we're lost and had better stop for directions." Their fear of losing control is evident in the frustration created by slow drivers, waiting in line for a movie or restaurant or postponing visits to the doctor.

Why do men prefer dogs over cats? Have you ever tried to control a cat? You cannot. Cats are incorrigible, and have independent character disorders! If you tell a dog to come to you, it will. Give a cat the same order, and it will stare at you, yawn, lie down or walk the other way. Control! Yes, it's an issue.

We fear being useless or unproductive, so we stay busy. We may see a purpose in our busyness even if no one else does.

Men fear losing their masculinity or sexual ability, so they hide behind jokes and off-color comments. We hide our fears of being needy and hurt by withdrawing and being even more silent. Our use of facts and logic as a way to live life and function well is a defense against the fear of facing emotions or having them overwhelm us so that we appear weak.[8]

Thus, when a man is encouraged to share his inner personal world, those making the request may not understand the extent of the fear they are confronting.

REACTIONS AND COMPENSATIONS

How do men react when their wives encourage—or require—them to share their feelings?

"She knows—or ought to know—how I feel. I really don't need to tell her, do I?"

"I'm just not sure how she will handle what I say. Yes, she likes to listen to the nice, positive, loving things. But when we discuss controversial subjects, she either gets upset, defensive, wants to know why I feel that way, talks about it forever or all of the above."

"I don't like responding to her question, 'Is that what you *really* mean?' or her comment, 'That doesn't make sense to me.'"

"If I don't say I love her or that I have missed her or that she looks pretty in the right way, she gets upset. When I do express these feelings, she responds with, 'Really?' or 'Do you mean it?' I just hate that. She seems to be questioning my sincerity. Why can't she accept my words at face value!"

"That's just me. That's the way I am. She may not like it, but that's me. I'm quiet. I think (she hates to hear that word) most men are, and I wish women would accept this fact. Just because I don't share a lot with her doesn't mean I don't love her. I do love her. I just don't want to get into unending discussions."

Men have learned clever techniques for withholding their feelings. The message they send to the world is that emotional expression and survival don't mix—and they believe it!

RESISTANCE AND DEFENSES

Resistance can wear many disguises.

Nonengagement is a form of resistance. The passive-aggressive approach works well for some men: "I don't know exactly what you want. Now, what is it that you want me to feel?"

Some men learn to express pseudo-feelings to fool others and to get what they want. They will say what other people want them to say so they can manipulate them.

A common defense is the use of intellect to guard against emotional expression. Intellect is used to filter emotional expression by creating flat responses devoid of feeling.

Some men share emotions in mixed messages. They prefer to let their emotions ooze out in nonverbal expressions.

Other men are very cynical about emotions. They say, "Feelings can't be trusted. They come and go; they're insincere. You can't trust them, so why bother?"

32

Unfortunately, too many men live (and die) by this creed. The results are described well by Dr. Gary Oliver in his insightful book *Real Men Have Feelings, Too.*

> By acting as if emotions and masculinity are incompatible, we have limited who God created us to be and become. The most devastating loss we have suffered by accepting these distortions is the loss of our hearts—the loss of our ability to feel, the ability to be tender as well as tough. We have lost the ability to be whole people.
>
> These myths have produced a generation of men who are significantly out of touch with what it means to have been created in the image of an infinite yet personal God. The myths have also produced a generation of men who have little idea of how to take care of themselves. Because men don't understand and know how to express their emotions, they don't know how to deal with emotional pain. Therefore, when we do have pain we don't understand it and don't know what to do with it, so our only option is to anesthetize it. If we don't feel, then we won't feel pain or fear or grief or loss.
>
> The anesthetic works for a while, but over time we need more and more. This leads to all kinds of destructive habits.[9]

33

Fortunately, there is hope. Not on the horizon, but now. Many men have a willingness to experience all of the manhood God has given to them. There is risk. There is confusion. There is gender misunderstanding on both sides. But the locks on the doors of the inner lives of many men are being unlocked—not by women, but by men themselves.

David Mains, a former pastor and host of radio's "Chapel of the Air," writes with refreshing candor about the big padlock on his emotions:

For a large part of my life I was tuned out emotionally. I wasn't aware of where others were coming from, and I didn't even understand my own feelings. I was probably extreme in that regard. I didn't know when I was tired. I seldom paid attention to whether I was hot or cold. I wasn't in touch with what I liked or didn't like. If someone would ask me what was wrong, instead of saying, "I feel trapped with no way out of this situation," I'd reply, "I'm OK, why do you ask?" Most of the time if someone accused me of expressing a negative emotion like anger or pride or frustration, I denied it. Was I stomping mad? No. Did I swear? Had my words stopped making sense because of my intense emotion? Never. What do you mean I was angry? You're accusing me of not acting the way a Christian should!

"You were emoting," my wife would tell me the next day. "It was as if you were sending out waves and waves of high voltage electricity. I don't understand how everybody can sense that except you."

Well, I wasn't in tune with my anger, my pain, my loneliness, my defensiveness, my fears, delights, moods, embarrassment, jealousies, whatever. I functioned relatively well in the objective world of ideas, facts, and words. But the more subjective realm of feeling was atrophying, shriveling up within me. Thank God that in recent years the Lord has been doing a major healing in me for which I'm extremely grateful. One of the signs of health is that my feelings are coming back into play.[10]

Where do we go from here? Into the private inner worlds of men to discover what they think and feel. Then to discover what both men and women can do to bring these private worlds out into daylight in positive ways so there will be new awareness, growth and blossoming of healthy relationships.

Reflecting on This Chapter

1. As a man, can you identify with the reasons for being reluctant to share feelings that are expressed in the quotation at the beginning of this chapter?
2. What is your age? Has your ability or willingness to share your inner life changed? For the better or worse? What brought about the change?
3. Define the following terms, and evaluate them in the light of their effect on relationships: (a) solitude, (b) privacy, (c) isolation, (d) remoteness, (e) quietness.
4. As a man, how do you relate to what Larry Crabb described as the feeling that there is an "empty place inside" or a "missing part"?
5. Do you agree with this chapter's analysis that many men fear the loss of control or power?
6. As a man, have you experienced a "turnaround" from reluctance to willingness to share your feelings? If so, describe the difference the change has made in your life.

Notes

1. H. Norman Wright, *Understanding the Man in Your Life* (Dallas: Word, Inc., 1987), p. 160.
2. Patrick Morley, *The Seven Seasons of a Man's Life* (Nashville: Thomas Nelson, 1995), p. 33.
3. Larry Crabb, *The Silence of Adam* (Grand Rapids: Zondervan Publishing House, 1995), pp. 11, 12.
4. Max Lucado, *Six Hours One Friday* (Dallas: Word, Inc., 1989), pp. 37, 38.
5. Verne Becker, *The Real Man Inside* (Grand Rapids: Zondervan Publishing House, 1992), p. 15.
6. Crabb, op. cit., p. 176.
7. Cited in Bill McCartney's, *What Makes a Man* (Colorado Springs: NavPress, 1992), p. 137.
8. Herb Goldberg, Ph.D., *What Men Really Want* (New York: Signet

Books, 1991), pp. 61-62, adapted.

9   Gary J. Oliver, *Real Men Have Feelings, Too* (Chicago: Moody Press, 1993), p. 37.

10. David Mains, *Healing the Dysfunctional Church Family* (Wheaton, Ill.: Victor Books, 1992), p. 123.

THE ENEMY WITHIN

You are thirsty and your throat is dry and parched. It feels as if it's cracking in places, like a desert floor. As your eyes scan the room, you notice a bowl of ripe, juicy, succulent oranges. You reach out and grab one, cut it in half, put it in the hand juicer and lower the lid. As you press down upon the lid, it begins to exert tremendous pressure on the orange. Your hand tires from the pressure, but you persevere until the last drop of orange juice is squeezed from the orange. Soon it is dry. Little or no moisture is left, and you discard the remains.

Some days you may feel like that orange; you are under so much pressure that at the end of the day not much is left of you.

PRESSURE FROM A HOSTILE WORLD

Pressure is one of the companions of modern man. A man who is a Christian lives in hostile territory. In many ways, he is imprisoned. Secular society is not neutral, instead it clamors to be exclusively secular and seeks to secularize all of its inhabitants. Christian opposition tries to convert us away from our faith, and their missionary efforts include many tactics.

Society would like nothing better than to reach out and imprison every Christian. Paul warns us of this challenge in his letter to the Colossians:

> See to it that no one takes you captive through hollow and deceptive philosophy, which depends on human tradition and the basic principles of this world rather than on Christ (2:8).

Our society says yes to everything. But our Christian view says yes only to God and His teaching. This external enemy can create incredible tension.

For many men there is an additional enemy—the internal enemy. R. C. Sproul describes it in notable words. "If a dog is man's best friend, perhaps his worst enemy is his mirror."

> Well, maybe his mirror isn't really his worst enemy; it merely reflects the image of his most formidable opponent. What opponent is more dangerous than the one who knows our deepest, darkest secrets? What opponent is more lethal than the one who can probe our most vulnerable points? The man in the mirror is me.[1]

Too often *we* are in many ways our own worst enemies.

IDENTITY AND A MAN'S CAREER

Creating our identities is one of our main struggles. Most men still base their identities on performance and production—what they are able to do. "Who am I?" may not always be a clearly asked question, but it is still a question that has driving force no matter what form it takes. Unfortunately, it typically remains related to the job.

Work today is unstable, therefore, major transitions are taking place and will continue to do so in the future. The work force is downsizing, limiting the variety and availability of jobs. Jobs are now geared more toward brains than brawn as information technology continues to surge ahead.

Many men in the prime of their lives are not out searching for new vocations, but available work of any sort. Some men have despaired and are not bothering to look.

Turning 50 is a risk because age and seniority are no longer a safety net. When you have invested four to six years in higher education to train for a profession and that profession (not just your company!) shrivels up, you may have no place to go. You are now "overqualified," thus, being well educated is no longer sufficient.

As men approach their 40s, the former daydream questions "How will I prepare for my next promotion and what will we do with the added benefits?" begin to reflect nightmarish concern as they ask, "How will I equip myself to start over if or when I'm out of a job? And how will we survive financially?" The seasoned professional often has nowhere to go.

Work and Meaning

Many men are facing a crisis of meaninglessness.[2] The writer of Ecclesiastes describes the turmoil for us:

> So I hated life, because the work that is done under the sun was grievous to me. All of it is meaningless, a chasing after the wind. I hated all the things I had toiled for under the sun, because I must leave them to the one who comes after me. And who knows whether he will be a wise man or a fool? Yet he will have control over all the work into which I have poured my effort and skill under the sun. This too is meaningless. So my heart began to despair over all my toilsome labor under the sun (2:17-20).

Most men and women don't understand the desperate, deep despair a job loss creates within a man. At first we cope, but the coping is like a balloon blown up to cushion the blow and portrays to others, "It's no big deal. I can handle it." Soon the balloon bursts. The explosion reveals the losses: financial loss, emotional loss and feelings of failure. Some men attribute their failure to their performance, whereas others see themselves as the failure.

A job loss is also traumatic for the younger man. It is true the veteran has more at stake, but at least he has a track record and knows what he can do. The younger man doesn't really know for sure what he can do yet. He is still testing and the opportunity to continue to do so is dissolved.

Take away a man's work and he's in trouble. His sense of purpose and the opportunity to do something constructive are woven into his thought processes and his perception of himself.[3] This is true of most Christian as well as non-Christian men.

This concern was evidenced again and again in our survey with men in response to the questions "What subject(s) do you think men hesitate most to bring up or discuss with women?" and "What is the greatest inner struggle that men deal with, but that women do not either know about or understand?"

The following are some of the responses related to these questions:

> Men are supposed to be the family leader, protector and spiritual leader. I admit that there are times that I am scared to death. What if I lose my job or can't pay the bills?

> The struggle to be "adequate" to define himself, to make some difference in the world.

> Work, worrying about being fired or laid off, incompetency, etc. Also getting older, relationship with the Lord. I think it revolves around the Lord. We need not fear these things if we know God.

> To trust God as provider and identity when the world pulls on me to trust only in myself to provide. The pulls of the world's values and economy versus God's economy and truth. Expectations from the world that I be successful.

For me, it's the issue of a sense of adequacy. I don't know about other men's inner struggles because I don't have too many men share them with me, even though I am a pastor.

The struggle to succeed. Not necessarily succeeding in amassing wealth, but in accomplishing something of value in his chosen profession. Men are competitive. That competition is also evident at work. We want to accomplish something in that realm. That brings satisfaction and a sense of worth to our lives.

More than a Job
Men do have a need for work, but work that is fulfilling and meaningful. Work *was and is* ordained by God. It is good. It is holy. It is a way to bring honor and glory to God.

Satan's influence and man's Fall messed up the plan. Work became harder:

> To Adam he said, "Because you listened to your wife and ate from the tree about which I commanded you, 'You must not eat of it,' Cursed is the ground because of you; through painful toil you will eat of it all the days of your life. It will produce thorns and thistles for you, and you will eat the plants of the field. By the sweat of your brow you will eat your food until you return to the ground, since from it you were taken; for dust you are and to dust you will return" (Gen. 3:17-19).

How would you feel about yourself if...

- You were the chief executive of a major country?
- You achieved tremendous success in business as an international trader?
- You were one of the richest men living?
- You constructed major shopping malls and

41

planned living communities?
- You contributed to your community by building parks, gardens and lakes?
- You were a gifted musician and writer?
- You commanded a great military force?

This is not a compilation of several men, but it is the resumé of one highly successful man. You know him; you have read about him; it is Solomon. Reflecting on all his past accomplishments, he wrote:

> I denied myself nothing my eyes desired; I refused my heart no pleasure. My heart took delight in all my work, and this was the reward for all my labor. Yet when I surveyed all that my hands had done and what I had toiled to achieve, everything was meaningless, a chasing after the wind; nothing was gained under the sun (Eccles. 2:10,11).

Despite all his achievements, Solomon wasn't satisfied. Why? Can you really be satisfied if your sole source of satisfaction is your work? Not really. A man is more than that! So is a woman.[4]

Identity as Relationship with Christ
When men struggle with identity and ask "*Who* am I?"—they are asking the wrong question. The right question is, "*Where* am I?" because that question points to our identity in relation to God Himself. Patrick Morley said, "We are who we are because of *where* we are."[5]

Many men hearing this take their task-oriented male perspectives and begin asking, "Then what can I start doing for God?" Again, wrong question. It is not doing things for God. It is simply being with Him.

If a man is task oriented in his relationship with God he will be asking, "What is the purpose of my life?" A more important question is, "*Who* is the purpose for my life?" That question focuses on a man's relationship with Jesus

Christ. By answering the second question first, the first question is easier to answer! Think about that![6]

Patrick Morley has written two informative and practical books for men. I highly recommend *The Man in the Mirror* and *The Seven Seasons of a Man's Life*. In the latter book, one unique chapter is a letter from God to a man. This insightful letter includes the following:

> You have wanted success. Success is elusive, isn't it? That's because you have been living by your own ideas. I do want you to be successful, but on My terms, not yours. You measure success in the quantity of your possessions and achievements. I measure success in the quality of your character and conduct. You are interested in the success of your goal. I am interested in the success of your soul. True success is to satisfy your calling, not your ambition. Live as a called man.
>
> The biggest problem I see in your life is that you have spent your whole life looking for something worth living for. It would be better if you found something worth dying for. Give your life to that, and I will give you joy, no matter how hard the path becomes. What is the cause you would be willing to die for? Better still, who is the one you would be willing to die for? How, then, should you reorder your life?
>
> I made you with dignity. I created you to be significant. I have put in you the spark of divinity. You are My crowning achievement. You are the full expression of My creative genius. You are My most excellent creation. I was at My very best when I created you. Do you understand and believe what I have just said?[7]

These statements should be read again and again. As they penetrate your value system about yourself, an attitude about how a Christian man is to form his identity—an attitude that at one time was perhaps an enemy—can become an ally.

43

MACHO MEN:
THE GREAT COVER-UP

The world's definition of "a real man" is an enemy to the identity God planned for men. If there is ever a place for the biblical admonition "Do not be conformed to this world" (Rom. 12:2, *NKJV*) to come into play, it is in this arena.

Perhaps the word that best describes this male struggle is "macho." It is a societal term that seems to be a goal for many men. It refers to the traditional male image taken to extremes. Its meaning is conveyed in the following four characteristics: (1) Avoid at all costs everything that even faintly resembles anything feminine, such as feelings, feeling words, tears, weakness, etc. (2) Achieve a status at all costs that means something to other men. (3) Make sure you appear tough, strong and, above all, independent. (4) Be as aggressive as you can be.

Macho is the great male cover-up. It is an extension of the hiding that began in the Garden when God came looking for Adam and Eve after they had disobeyed Him. This image that men foster and project is not only rooted somewhat in genetic male characteristics, but also largely developed by what is taught, portrayed and reinforced in our society. We have developed unrealistic cultural role models in films, TV, sports and literature that capture the attention and adulation of men.

Men are still being taught to compete, but competition is not the problem. The problem is winning at any cost, at the expense of others no matter what. Men are taught by other men and society not to need anyone, to be independent. They are told not to appear weak. Men are taught that task attainment and completion are more important than developing a relationship. "And above all, don't ask for help."

In *Men: A Book for Women*, these cultural tendencies are described as follows:

> He shall not cry.
> He shall not display weakness.

He shall not need affection or gentleness or
    warmth.
He shall comfort but not desire comforting.
He shall be needed but not need.
He shall touch but not be touched.
He shall be steel not flesh.
He shall be inviolate in his manhood.
He shall stand alone.[8]

A macho man is one who tries too hard to live up to our society's false standards for manhood. If he does attain them, he is unable to relate to others because he has become hardened and unresponsive to the needs of others. He has become powerful. He makes his own choices.

Isn't it interesting that the one Man who had the ability to be the most powerful Man in the world chose instead to be meek, to be a servant and to minister to the hurting? What does Christ's model say to those of us who follow Him—or who say they do?

The Lust for Control

When men become powerful they also tend to become controlling. Control is disastrous in the working world and in marriage. In the insightful book *When Love Dies: The Process of Marital Dissatisfaction*, the author spells out in detail the process in which couples fall out of love. It is a predictable process. In the chapter "What Causes Love to Die," the majority of the respondents indicated that it was a spouse's attempt to control them that created the turning point in the marriage. This was often called "emotional abuse and domination."[9]

More than 1,500 years ago, Augustine expressed the ideal of a husband-wife relationship:

> If God meant woman to rule over man, He would have taken her out of Adam's head. Had He designed her to be his slave, He would have taken her out of his feet. But God took woman out of man's side, for He made her to be a helpmeet and an equal to him.[10]

The Untouchable Male

The macho male strives to portray an image of invulnerability. It's an image of a house without doors, a castle without a drawbridge, a man who cannot be touched. Men become like certain animals.

> A peacock raises its tail feathers to scare off attackers. It is a behavior meant to disguise weakness and vulnerability. A turtle retreats into the dense defense of its shell. Men often behave like the peacock or the turtle. If we are in danger of being found out, we will fan our achievements and wield a display of power, or we will retreat into our impenetrable fortresses. Either way our manly image remains intact. We are proud creatures.[11]

The macho image is contradictory to the Christian man's calling because it puts *him* rather than *God* at the center of his universe. The authors of *Man and Woman, Alone and Together* state the macho problem this way:

> It fosters distance and impersonality, rationality at the expense of sensitivity, and the effort to protect oneself at the expense of membership in the body of believers. Because it is so highly valued in society, we accept this myth in the church. We look for "strong leaders," "powerful men of God," "machos for the Master." We give such men higher status in the church, forgetting the Good Shepherd and the "widow's mite," forgetting that the powerful God we see in the Old Testament is the same one who promises to comfort Israel "as a mother" (Isa. 66:13).[12]

The macho mystique leads to isolation and death—there is no other way to put it. Close friendships? As one man said, "Close friends? No, I don't have any. Why? Do I need them?"

Stu Weber, in his book *Tender Warrior*, describes the struggle many men face:

Oh, we may *want* that friendship. Every man, whether he admits it or not, walks around with a hollow place in his chest, wondering if he is the only one. But there is something within us that keeps us at arm's length. *What is that something that keeps men distant and friendless?*

I saw a man about my age the other day in a crowded parking lot. If one Vietnam vet can spot another, then I knew this man for what he was and what he had endured. I felt an immediate love for him. He was on crutches, and one pant leg was folded and pinned up to the top. Everyone in that busy lot seemed to avert their eyes from this disabled gentleman. It's something we find ourselves doing in that sort of situation, isn't it? One glance tells us something isn't normal. Something isn't right. Something's missing. In the physical sense, this man wasn't "all there."

I think most of us would have to admit that when it comes to open and vulnerable man-to-man friendships, we are walking on one leg. We're really not "all there." Something's missing. Something's pinned up and empty in our souls. We may be "kings" and "warriors," but we seem to have lost something of the tender side. So we're really one-legged men. We simply don't know how to fellowship.[13]

TOWARD A NEW MEASURE OF MANHOOD

It is difficult (but not impossible) for men to change. Admitting that the pursuit of the macho image is not the best choice is difficult, and to risk being different is to invite ridicule. The loss of status in the eyes of other men is a fear that can limit progress.

There is also the fear, "I'll lose my masculinity. I'll be soft, passive, a pushover."

No, the calling to be a Christian man is anything but soft

and passive. Christianity embodies all of the genuine male characteristics in a balanced and healthy way. Man becomes more masculine in Christ, not less.

The Tender Warrior

The best description I have seen of ideal manhood is from a book written by Stu Weber, a pastor and former Green Beret who served in Vietnam. His book *Tender Warrior* is one of the four best books I know of for men, and I would encourage all men to read it. (See the recommended reading list at the end of this chapter).

In his book Stu talks about being a warrior, a tender warrior rather than a "soft male." It is no wonder that men do not view "soft" as a positive quality. Do you know what the dictionary says about soft? It is "Giving way easily under pressure, bland, weak, delicate, not strong, not able to endure hardship, kind to the point of weakness, easily imposed upon."[14]

That is not a positive description for a man.

A tender warrior is just the opposite. The word "tender" means "to express love, compassion, and kindness; affectionate, careful, considerate, gentle, and mild, not harsh or heavy."[15] Paul described his own response in this way: "Our attitude among you was one of tenderness" (1 Thess. 2:7, *Phillips*).

This man was tender and gentle. He said:

> We proved to be gentle among you, as a nursing mother tenderly cares for her own children. Having thus a fond affection for you, we were well-pleased to impart to you not only the gospel of God but also our own lives, because you had become very dear to us (1 Thess. 2:7,8, *NASB*).

This is the same man who endured more suffering than you and I will ever experience:

> I have worked harder than any of them. I have served more prison sentences! I have been beaten

times without number. I have faced death again
and again. I have been beaten the regulation thir-
ty-nine stripes by the Jews five times. I have been
beaten with rods three times. I have been stoned
once. I have been shipwrecked three times. I have
been twenty-four hours in the open sea. In my
travels I have been in constant danger from rivers
and floods, from bandits, from my own country-
men, and from pagans. I have faced danger in the
city streets, danger in the desert, danger on the
high seas, danger among false Christians. I have
known exhaustion, pain, long vigils, hunger and
thirst, doing without meals, cold and lack of clothing (2 Cor. 11:23-27, *Phillips*).

The Balance Jesus Offers

What then is God's word for men today? It is that we should
be balanced men. How do we live balanced lives? By fixing
our eyes on Jesus, the author and finisher of our faith. Jerry
Johnson describes it best:

> Jesus' personality had several facets, but he did
> not hide them from anyone. He could chase the
> corrupters out of his temple in righteous anger,
> displaying his manhood in what might be called
> "masculine" ways—and yet later he wept over
> Jerusalem, displaying what is considered a "femi-
> nine" side.
>
> He met the challenge of the enemy and faced
> them in open debate; and yet he could hold chil-
> dren on his knees and in a moment of tenderness
> express how precious they were to him and to the
> kingdom of God.
>
> He walked the bloody highways of Palestine,
> littered with the flotsam of man's inhumanity to
> man, pursued, harassed and carrying a price on
> his head; and yet he could sit and allow a woman
> to wash his feet and dry them with her hair, and
> rebuke those who thought it inappropriate.

On more than one occasion, he lashed out with a sharp verbal lance, even calling the religious leaders a bunch of "vipers," thus taking the wind right out of them and leaving them dumbfounded; and yet he dealt mercifully with a frantic father who honestly confessed his inability to believe that Jesus could heal his son, touching the boy in tenderness, compassion and power—making him whole.

He had all the legions of heaven on his side and could have, in one master stroke of his manliness, wiped out his enemies. Yet he stood mute before the Roman court, refusing to give dignity to a mob.

Here is the Son of God, Jesus, the Man, who was not asexual, but who never used his sexuality to prove his manhood.

Here is the king of the universe, sweating blood during the deep revulsion he felt in Gethsemane concerning the death that faced him, and yet pressing on to take that death on the cross without wilting.

There is no greater picture of the "whole man"— man who was "masculine" in terms of strength, muscle, sinew and courage and yet was not ashamed to show his "feminine" side in terms of tears, compassion, gentleness and peace. He said, "I must finish the task," which in essence means, "I must win for humanity the redemption God designed through me." He won that redemption in the end on the strength of his total manhood, which was beautiful, dynamic and sensitive.[16]

The Need for a New Vision

Men today need a new perspective, a new vision of all they can become. One of my favorite Bible verses is in the book of Joel: "Your old men will dream dreams, your young men will see visions" (2:28). When you have a vision for what you want to become and do in the future, you are able to move upstream against the difficult currents that hit you in the face again and again. When you see things as they could be, you need not let the odds overwhelm you. You will recognize obstacles, but you won't dwell upon them.

Vision is the ability to focus on God's plan for you for the future, regardless of the problems. It is looking at life through God's eyes to see the potential He can see.

Worse than being lost is the failure to admit that you are lost. You keep doing the same things again and again, running around in the same circles, never getting anywhere, like the cast in J. R. R. Tolkien's fantasy story *The Hobbit*. A band of dwarves and one little hobbit are wandering around lost in a dismal forest. Other creatures had warned them about this place, but they were hungry and decided to wander around. Now they were lost and in deep danger. They were thirsty and hungry, and all around were huge, deadly spiders. They couldn't find their way out because of the height and density of the forest. They couldn't see the sky through the foliage.

So the dwarves sent Bilbo the hobbit up an old tree to see if he could discover where they were and find a way out. He climbed and climbed, and as he climbed the branches got smaller and smaller. Soon he was at the top and finally able to thrust his head above the last leaves. He was startled by the dazzling sunlight and the clear sky. The rotting smell of the damp forest was gone and he could breathe fresh air. He could see!

We can see, too, if we stick our heads above the macho jungle and catch a vision of what we as men can become.

God's Word can give direction:

> If any of you lacks wisdom, he should ask God,
> who gives generously to all without finding fault,
> and it will be given to him (Jas. 1:5).

A man does not destroy his masculinity by rejecting the false macho persona, he enhances it. Masculinity is a healthy expression of the design of God's creation. A macho man has distorted masculinity. The behaviors of a macho man are a cover-up for fear and insecurity. Becoming aggressive, controlling and power hungry distances other people so they won't discover our inner insecurities.

A truly masculine man accepts the uniqueness of who he

is and is open to developing underdeveloped areas of his life. He is a lifelong student of himself. He is flexible and adaptable. He does not fear change; he embraces it.

CHRIST, OUR HOPE FOR THE FUTURE

How does all this happen? Through Jesus, that's how. Jesus Christ can reconstruct and restore our inner man and set us free to be all that God intended us to be. When this occurs, many issues will be resolved and personal and family relationships will have the opportunity to become the way they were intended to be.

As we continue to dissect the private lives of men, the one word to remember is "hope." Admittedly the need is urgent. Both men and women need a greater level of understanding, acceptance and growth. But there is hope. Our outlooks, beliefs and relationships may need to change; and with God's help they can.

To help you move toward the future with hope, I invite you to consider some words that have helped me tremendously. In Roger Palms's penetrating devotional book entitled *Enjoying the Closeness of God*, he says:

> In Christ I am free to live, free to be flexible, free to move, free to fail, free to succeed. I can confidently know that there are things I will do well and things that I will not be able to do at all. I don't have to try to prove to myself or to others that somehow I can be what I am not. God made me; God owns me.
>
> And as I relax in Christ, I begin to see that there have always been people like me. This reinforces my certainty. I meet people in Scripture—people like Abraham, Moses, Stephen—who did not fully understand themselves or their purpose but they knew that God understood them. They did not always feel strong or healthy or wise. They wondered at God's commands as sometimes I do. Even the disciple who loved Jesus most didn't always

understand everything He did or taught. Realizing this allows me to have moments of depression; it allows me to cry and pound my fists on God's chest. It allows me to be the person I am because I am God's person. I can look to my Creator because I am His. I can look to my Redeemer; I can look ahead to fulfillment and to deliverance. And I can be happy even in my "failures," waiting to see how these too will be used because I am secure in the One who made me and owns me.

I know that there is a tomorrow.[17]

RECOMMENDED READING

Morley, Patrick M. *The Man in the Mirror*. Brentwood, Tenn.: Wolgemuth & Hyatt, 1989.
Morley, Patrick M. *The Seven Seasons of a Man's Life*. Nashville: Thomas Nelson, 1995.
Oliver, Gary J. *Real Men Have Feelings, Too*. Chicago: Moody Press, 1993.
Weber, Stu. *Tender Warrior*. Sisters, Oreg.: Questar, 1993.

REFLECTING ON THIS CHAPTER

1. What pressures do you think society places on you that may threaten your Christian commitment?
2. As a man, are you aware of pressures you put on yourself that may not be helpful for relationships?
3. Do you think that you, as a man, define who you are by what you do? (One way to answer this question is to ask yourself how you would feel if you lost your present job and had to seek another.)
4. Have you had the experience of being laid off from work, or passed over for a promotion that went to a younger person? If so, how did you handle it?
5. Do you agree or disagree with the author's claim that "Macho is the great male cover-up"?
6. What specific traits of Jesus would you wish for all men?

Notes

1. Patrick M. Morley, *The Man in the Mirror* (Brentwood, Tenn.: Wolgemuth & Hyatt, 1989), p. xi.
2. Gail Sheehy, *New Passages* (New York: Random House, 1995), pp. 68, 69, 248, adapted.
3. John Munder Ross, *The Male Paradox* (New York: Simon & Schuster, 1992), pp. 179, 183, adapted.
4. Patrick M. Morley, *The Seven Seasons of a Man's Life* (Nashville: Thomas Nelson, 1995), pp. 58-59, adapted.
5. Ibid., p. 145.
6. Ibid., pp. 144-145, adapted.
7. Ibid., pp. 151-152.
8. James Wagenvoord, ed., *Men: A Book for Women* (New York: Avon Books, 1978), p. 105.
9. Karen Kayser, *When Love Dies* (New York: The Guilford Press, 1993), pp. 93-96, adapted.
10. As quoted in Dwight Hervey Small's *After You've Said "I Do"* (Grand Rapids: Fleming H. Revell, 1968), pp. 50-51.
11. Tom L. Eisenman, *Temptations Men Face* (Downers Grove, Ill.: InterVarsity Press, 1991), p. 38.
12. Kaye Cook and Lance Lee, *Man and Woman, Alone and Together* (Wheaton, Ill.: Victor Books, 1992), p. 76.
13. Stu Weber, *Tender Warrior* (Sisters, Oreg.: Questar, 1993), p. 174.
14. *Webster's New World Dictionary* (New York: Prentice Hall, 1994), p. 1274.
15. Ibid., p. 1378.
16. Jerry Johnson, *What Every Woman Should Know About a Man* (Grand Rapids: Zondervan Publishing House, 1981), pp. 104-105.
17. Roger C. Palms, *Enjoying the Closeness of God* (Minneapolis: World Wide Publications, 1989), p. 246.

COPING
WITH LOSSES
LIKE A MAN

The losses of men are a window.

Windows allow us to see inside a structure. A large picture window that has clear, undistorted glass provides an unobstructed view of the building's interior.

Loss is that window providing a clear understanding of the previously identified characteristics of most men.

Loss is not a favorite topic for discussion or thought. So why do we include loss in a book about the private lives of men? Because for most men it is just that—private. And the characteristics of loss reflect many of the concerns raised about men.

"Loss" is a simple, four-letter word representative of a constant undesired companion in the lives of all men. Loss violates one of man's basic beliefs: "I'm in control and I must succeed."

GREAT EXPECTATIONS

Our society reinforces the valuelessness of loss. Look at the headlines on the sports page. To whom are the accolades given? Not to the losers. When you lose, it hurts. The world makes room for winners, not losers. Whether a loss is small or large, it hurts. It carries a message of failure. Loss implies you haven't succeeded in being a "man." Even the normal transitional losses of life are uncomfortable to face and admit.

Those who recover from losses and gain strength through them are those who learn to grieve about their losses.

Why does a man respond to loss the way he does?

He is *expected* to respond in a particular way.

He is *predisposed* to respond in a particular way.

He is *physically capable* of responding in a particular way.[1]

Look at the pressure of our cultural expectations. A man is expected to be confident and assertive—not afraid, hesitant, anxious, insecure or sad.

He is expected to be sufficient, know what he is doing, be rational and analytical, not passive, dependent, bewildered or in need of support or comfort.

Most men are well aware of these expectations and try to live up to them. They guard against becoming what society says they must *not be*.

Other factors also create tension during times of loss. Many men were raised emotionally handicapped in their abilities to express their inner responses. Most women grow up with rich vocabularies for their emotions; but much of men's energies are directed toward withholding or denying socially disfavored emotions. Men invest their energies in *not being* the way God intended them to be, which creates tension and stress.

Because men are supposed to be competitors, every loss shouts the message, "You didn't make it!" Even when men don't have much control over the outcome, the inner message is loud and clear. Any association with something that doesn't work brands men with the stigma of losing. If a teenage son succumbs to peer pressure and rebels, his rebellion is a negative reflection on the father. He couldn't control his child. Somehow he failed as a dad.

If a man is on a team of lawyers prosecuting a major case, the verdict of "not guilty" labels them as the losing team. Even the background research attorneys on the team have to face the stigma of having lost, although factors beyond their control (jurors or lack of accurate police work) destroyed their chances from the outset.

MALE RESPONSES TO LOSS

How do men usually respond to their losses? How else but in ways that conform to society's prescription for "real men"?

The Silent Treatment
Most men keep their feelings *and* thoughts bottled up. A quiet, introverted man is even more likely to react this way.

Men tend to think their way through circumstances, whereas women talk their way through them. Thinking is done alone. Talking involves others. When you think alone, you never really discover what you are troubled about because there is no explaining; questions that are asked are not answered and no one else helps to figure out what you cannot figure out by yourself.

Most men tend not to share their problems with their friends. Women lighten the load by sharing the weight, whereas men get emotional hernias by carrying the load themselves.[2]

One result of this trait is that other people don't ask men about their feelings when they experience losses. Instead, they may ask a man how his wife and children are doing. They expect that he is able to handle it like a man.

Few people ever asked how I was doing when they learned that our son was mentally retarded. Fortunately, when Matthew died, people asked me as much as Joyce about my feelings. Think about it. When a couple experiences a miscarriage, is the husband ever asked how he is doing? Not usually.

When a child is seriously ill, is the father asked what he needs or how he is holding up? Not usually.

Many of the losses we as men experience have no opportunity to be discussed because they are neither recognized as losses nor shared with anyone else.

Too often the messages (including avoidance) a man

receives verbally and nonverbally reinforce the expectation, "You're not going to get all emotional on me now, are you? You're not going to be vulnerable or afraid or cry or show me weakness, are you?"

Why not? Why should we struggle to respond differently from the way God created us?

If the comment is made, "This must be pretty rough on you," a man may respond with "Uh-huh, yeah"—and nothing more, because he may not know how to describe what is going on inside, or it may be too uncomfortable. Other typical responses are, "Oh, I'm making it all right" or, "I can handle it."

When I talk to men about their losses and receive those kind of responses, I ask a second question: "But, how do you really feel about it?" Then they usually open up because they have been given a sincere invitation to express their feelings.

In talking to a depressed man who had been divorced eight years earlier by his first wife, I received a stoic stare when I suggested that perhaps his current difficulties were based on his not grieving about that previous loss. The statement had hit too close to home. His face softened and his response was, "That's it exactly. I guess I've never really come to grips with that."

Although he was now six years into a new family and had a stable marriage, he agreed to go through a divorce recovery group. Afterward, he couldn't praise the experience enough for how it had helped him. He finally learned to grieve his loss, and in that way became more fully alive in all areas of his life.

Perhaps the struggle is best depicted by the following statement, which reflects the pattern of our culture:

> In our culture men are taken seriously because they *don't* talk about their feelings. Women are not taken seriously because they are so open about their feelings.[3]

One of the most graphic and sad descriptions of what results when a man doesn't face his loss and grief is described in a novel by Frederick Forsyth titled *The Negotiator*. A president's son had been kidnapped. The father had experienced the trauma of not knowing where his son was, what condition he was in or whether he would ever be freed. Then the son was brutally murdered. Afterward, cabinet members were worried about the president. He sat and stared into space:

> Too introverted a man to share easily, too inhibited to express his grief, he had settled into an abiding melancholy that was sapping his mental and moral strength, those qualities humans call the will.[4]

Grieving Alone, Hiding Tears

A second way men handle grief is by going it alone. Men often give excuses for what they are doing or why they were not at work rather than openly saying, "I was so overcome with grief over the loss that I wasn't able to function or help anyone. I was hurting."

Sometimes men grieve alone to avoid burdening others, although they have been known to open up to strangers. Grieving alone fits many of the cultural expectations for the way men are "supposed" to behave. Therefore, the emotions of grief are a constant challenge to a man.

Men grieve alone to avoid weeping in front of others. Newspaper reports of tragedies often do not bother to say that a woman was weeping, because that is expected. The reports will tell about it if a man was crying, however, because men are not expected to cry. A spoken and unspoken message says that if a man cries, his tears should be confined to a funeral home or hospital, not out in public.

If a person starts to cry in a hospital corridor or waiting room, a nurse or doctor will say, "We have a room over here that you can use for crying. You'll be more comfortable there." Hospital personnel may not be as concerned about the comfort level of the grief-stricken person as they are about their own comfort, and that of others who may be present. Especially if a man cries in public, other people are usually uncomfortable and want to stop him.[5]

Some men have never learned to cry outwardly. They cry only on the inside. Listen to the words of a father who lost a newborn daughter:

> I called Steve.
> "We had a daughter, early," I told him. "We named her Kim. She's dead." And I cried.
> Steve listened. He didn't say much either. But when he did, he asked, "How are you?"
> Strange question. No one else seemed to care. To know. To think that men feel loss as much as women do. But I can hurt, and so few people seem to understand that. Most acquaintances express condolences and then ask, "How is Cynthia taking it?"
> Fine, I guess. She's got me. And her women friends. And her mother. And the sympathy of everyone else in the whole world. Why is there an assumption that I don't bleed inside? That men don't hurt? We do hurt. We are vulnerable. We do feel. And even if we don't admit it, we tend to resent it when nobody asks. But we try not to show hurt. We have crying rooms down the hall where we can let it out and then "be strong" for those who need us.
> Earlier...the physician had pointed to a small room down the hall and told me it was mine if I wanted it. A crying room. A man's fortress of solitude.[6]

Recently I was talking with a couple about their upcoming move to a new area of the country. The 54-year-old man said that when he told his good friend and business associate about his move, he broke down. My response was, "That's an interesting statement—'I broke down.' Cars 'break down.' Was this something that needed to be fixed?"

Because he is a man who openly shares and talks about his feelings he said, "No. I don't know why I said that. I cried in front of him and that's all right."

When we use phrases such as "he broke down," we perpetuate the unhealthiness of our culture. When Scripture talks about Jesus weeping, it says simply, "Jesus wept."

I think one of the most significant statements about tears was written by Max Lucado. As he put it, "When words are most empty, tears are most apt."[7] I, too, had to learn this.

When General Schwarzkopf was interviewed after the Gulf War by Barbara Walters, his eyes teared up as they were looking at pictures of his family. Barbara Walters said, "Generals don't cry."

Schwarzkopf replied, "Sure, they do, Barbara. Grant cried after Shiloh; Sherman went back and cried; Lee cried at the loss of human life. Frankly, any man who doesn't cry scares me a little bit."

After we learned the severity of our son's retardation, I didn't cry about it for months. I still had a sense of disbelief. One evening about 10 months later, however, we were watching a television show called "Then Came Bronson," in which the main character traveled around the country on a motorcycle. In this particular episode, Bronson worked at a ranch for autistic children who could not speak. He worked with one child day after day and week after week. At the end of the program, the child spoke one word.

When I saw that, it was as though a key had unlocked a vault door holding back all my pain. As I felt the flood coming, I quickly left the room (the old message was intact: "don't cry in front of anyone"). I went to the kitchen, and wept by myself. Fortunately, Joyce came in and held me so we could grieve together. We men need our turn to grieve, no matter what the loss.

In his book *Fight Like a Man*, Gordon Dalbey said believing that "real men don't cry" has cost us men dearly. It has cut us off from our own selves, from others and from God. For God's warriors, the consequences are grave. Dalbey writes: "The weeping willow bends and survives the storm intact; the hard oak cracks and falls."[8]

"Doing Something About It"
Another way men deal with their losses is by taking action. It

might be doing something physical, or suing someone. When a job is lost, doing something about it can be helpful, perhaps resulting in a new job. Even small losses elicit this response unless a man is immobilized by depression.

Part of this drive to take action stems from our need to try to take back some control when a loss occurs. Our culture expects action, and action is one of our pillars of security. A loss wrestles control away from us, and in some way we want it back. So why not *act* to do so?

When a man confronts the feeling of helplessness by taking action, his anger becomes evident because anger provides the energy that spurs the action. Angry action is graphically seen in the grief responses of Vietnam veterans who lost friends or portions of their own bodies in the war.

When children are injured or killed, rage about this tragedy and loss is best vented through constructive action.

There is also a downside to angry action. It can obscure a man's thoughts and behavior so much that emotions such as sadness, despair or longing have no opportunity to be felt and faced. Further, the expression of a man's anger can become outwardly destructive or, if turned back upon himself, do internal damage. It can keep him from responding to his wife's grief. He, therefore, grieves in solitude rather than with his spouse.

The search for blame during times of loss can lead to lashing out with lawsuits against businesses, schools, doctors, hospitals or whatever or whomever we believe might have been negligent.

In a major loss such as a family death, it is often difficult to take action because most of the "action" activities related to the loss are "subcontracted." Think about it—what is there *to do*? The "death professionals" take charge—building and providing the coffin, organizing the service, digging the grave, obtaining the flowers and even driving to the funeral. It is difficult for a man to stand around and have nothing to do when the opportunity for activity has been taken away.

For some, rigorous physical activity can result in healing. The need to engage in such activities produces unique responses as various personalities try to cope with loss. I heard about a man who had lost his father in a tragic fire. He lived near his father on an adjacent farm. One night the home in which he was born and raised burned to the ground and his father was inside. The man's response to this tragedy startled other family members. He remained silent, while they wept and talked about the loss.

After a rain had extinguished the fire, the man borrowed a bulldozer and proceeded to bulldoze the ashes and charred remains of the house. This action was how he expressed his need to bury his father. He worked for hours, not stopping for meals or rest. When darkness fell he continued, ignoring the requests of family members to stop for the night. He continued to bulldoze the remains back and forth, again and again.

This man and his father were farmers and for most of their lives had worked together in the fields. They didn't verbalize much together nor share feelings; but they had a close, nonverbal relationship.

Some may grieve with tears, but this man grieved with a borrowed bulldozer. Taking this kind of action was his own personal expression of words and tears. He "cried" by working the land over and over again until nothing was visible. He gave his father and the home a proper burial, but in his own way. The land, which in a sense was his father's cemetery, was now ready to be farmed—and the son would be the one to do it. If you were to ask this man why he had done this, he could not give you an answer. He didn't know why, but he did something with his grief and it was probably the best thing he could have done.[9]

Cultural Acts of Grieving
It's interesting to note both the differences and the similarities in the way men act out their grief in various cultures.

In some societies such as the Bara people in Madagascar, men and women actually separate from each other following a death. A "male hut" is designated for men and a "house of tears" for women. The latter is the place of emotional expression, but the male house is the center of action where the men work out the details of the funeral ritual.

Other cultures actually give men active tasks. In Africa the

Dagura men dance out the life of the person who died. Other cultures have the men sing about the life of the dead person.[10]

In the United States, examples of action are reflected in Eric Clapton's song about his son who died. Through his gift of music, Clapton found a way to grieve in his pain. Abraham Lincoln was said to invite a friend to the White House to play what he called "sad songs." They sat in the same room where his son had died, and as the friend played the piano Lincoln would sit and cry. The songs became Lincoln's way of tapping into his feelings. This is what all of us need—a way to access what is churning around inside.

For some men, just doing something—anything—is a way of grieving. As a wife in counseling expressed it, "It's like he is on a treadmill. I wish he would sit still for a while. He just goes and goes and goes. And when I suggest that he cut back, he says it hurts too much when he does nothing."

When the news of a serious loss first hits a man, he may throw himself with fervor into work and household activity in an attempt to overcome the feelings of powerlessness and pain. His hours at work may increase, or he may become obsessive in fixing up the house. The increased activity is noticeable to others by its intensity.

If the man is already a workaholic or a type A personality, his activity level is often frenzied. The constant motion is similar to that of a hyperactive child who never runs down. Once again, the activity hinders dealing with his true feelings. It is a discomfort-blocking technique. Every man has a need to feel, whether he knows it or not. He needs to learn that feelings are a normal part of life.

When my son, Matthew, was admitted to the hospital in March 1990, two weeks prior to his death, I decided to paint the house. Why just then? It needed painting, but I could have begun anytime. Only later did I realize that there was a definite purpose in my timing.

Unfortunately, some men may cross the boundary of healthful activity and move into risk taking—such as driving fast, scuba diving or drinking excessively. Engaging in addictive behavior is yet another expression of grief associated with losses.

Avoidance and Fear

Another response can be expected from a man who suffers a significant loss. He will do everything possible *not* to show his fear or insecurity. We men don't do well admitting our fears.

Years ago, I learned to ask my counselees (male and female), "What is the fear in your life that drives you?" I was amazed at the extent of fear I uncovered. Most of us are more driven by fear than drawn by hope. Our behavior certainly doesn't reflect fear, but often it could be prompted by fear.

One of the common male fears is: *If I show despair or depression, how do I know that eventually I'll be OK? What will keep it from going on and on?* I like what I hear in this message from a grief therapist to a grieving man:

> If you are among those who feel that you do not know how intense, lengthy, or deep your expression of grief may be, you may find yourself thinking that it would be impossible—or at least very difficult—for you to pull out of grief's deep pit to do all the things you need to do before or after the death. Being afraid of getting sucked down into a hollow of "no return" is not realistic. *Grief is not quicksand. Rather, it is a walk on rocky terrain that eventually smoothes out and proves less challenging— both emotionally and physically.* So if you find yourself fearful of grieving, if you're imagining the worst or expecting some untenable transformation to take place within yourself, try putting those catastrophic thoughts in their proper perspective.
>
> For example, you may think: *I will fall apart and won't be able to function if I start to show how I feel.* Replace such a thought with the more realistic: I will let go for a time, release what I feel, and will be able to function better as a result of having vented the feelings that are an ever-present burden.
>
> You may think: *If I let myself grieve, then I will change permanently and won't ever be able to be myself again.* It's a fact that grief changes most survivors whether or not they vent their emotions

65

and express their feelings. You can't keep change
from happening after a loss; it is part of surviving
a death. But you can take control over the type of
change you experience. As you allow yourself to
grieve, the changes that take place will be ones
which allow you to go forward, to integrate loss,
and to resolve the issues related to your loved
one's death. Venting your responses can be like
turning a searchlight on something moving in the
shadows—which you imagine to be more enormous and menacing that it really is. Once the light
is on, your caution seems to have been completely
unnecessary.[11]

The ways men grieve simply point out once again the differences between men and women. Are these ways of grieving wrong? No man would admit or want to admit they are
wrong, or even inadequate. Let's just say there are better and
healthier ways to adjust, cope and grow.

Sharing our feelings and loss with others is a better way.
Some men have asked, "But how can men do this if they are
wired and trained *not* to be this way?" Perhaps the answer is
that a time of loss may be the opportune time to become different. It is a time to realize, "I am not in control of my life; I
don't have all the answers; I have an abundance of different
feelings; my beliefs that *it isn't safe to share and real men don't
cry* may not be accurate—there just may be a different and
better way to live.

Once such realizations take root, the door opens for
growth and a different way of living, which can be much better than the way we are living now.

REFLECTING ON THIS CHAPTER

1. Why is it often difficult for men to deal with loss?
2. Do you think most men are more competitive than
most women? Is competitiveness a negative aspect
in your marriage?
3. As a man, do you recall any incidents from your

youth when it was communicated that "big boys don't cry"? If so, do you think it's a handicap?

4. Do you think demands on men to be "tough" on the job often affect their home lives? Do you think the increased number of women working outside the home in recent years has resulted in their taking on more of this "masculine" trait?

5. Are you aware of any fears in yourself or others that may underlie an "upbeat" exterior? What are some healthy ways to deal with fear?

6. Do you and your spouse differ in the way you express grief?

Notes

1. Carol Staudacher, *Men and Grief* (Oakland, Calif.: New Harbinger Publications, 1991), pp. 19-38, adapted.
2. Michael McGill, *The McGill Report on Male Intimacy* (New York: HarperCollins, 1985), p. 176, adapted.
3. Staudacher, op. cit., p. 155, adapted.
4. Frederick Forsyth, *The Negotiator* (New York: Bantam Books, 1989), p. 269.
5. Staudacher, op. cit., pp. 22, 25, adapted.
6. Roger Witherspoon, "Say Brother," *Essence* 14:5 (1983).
7. Max Lucado, *No Wonder They Call Him Savior* (Portland, Oreg.: Multnomah Press, 1986), p. 106.
8. Gordon Dalbey, *Fight Like a Man* (Wheaton, Ill.: Tyndale House, 1995), p. 235.
9. Ann Kaiser Stearns, *Living Through Personal Crisis* (New York: Ballantine Books, 1984), pp. 65-66, adapted.
10. Tom Golden, "Gender Differences in Grief," *Bereavement—A Magazine of Hope and Healing,* 9 (May/June 1995): 7, adapted.
11. Staudacher, op. cit., p. 150.

EMOTIONAL
EVASION AND
ITS COST

They first noticed each other in a college class where they struck up a conversation. Soon they were sitting next to each other; then one day they went out to dinner. The dating process began and continued after graduation. They talked about everything, or so it seemed. That was 10 years ago. Today, after 8 years of marriage and two children, they seldom talk. Hear their story.

"When Jim and I were dating we got along so well. I mean, we could talk. There didn't seem to be any restrictions. My questions were always answered and Jim appeared to be interested in everything. Sure, we both knew I tended to talk more than he did, but that didn't *seem* to be a problem. I didn't have to push him to talk.

"A month after we married, however, our communication changed. I did not change—he did. He began to respond with about a tenth of his previous openness, and it continues. He has become so private. I know I have made mistakes. I've pressured him and talked more. I have tried to figure him out but it hasn't worked. Did I do something wrong to turn him off? How could a man communicate so well during courtship and then pull the plug after we married? Was it a play to win me? I feel deceived, disappointed, set up."

BLENDING VERSUS COLLIDING

When a man and woman marry, there should be a blending and meshing of two individuals into a complementary union. Marriage is a fusion of two personalities, but each retains an individual identity.

The *ideal* has been described with the following analogy. If you were to hold a lump of dark green clay in one hand and a lump of light green clay in the other, you would clearly see the different shades. But if you were to take both pieces of clay and mold and push them together, at first glance you would see just one lump of green clay. Close inspection of the lump would reveal the distinct and separate lines of dark and light clay.

Marriage was intended to be like the clay—two people blended and functioning well together, while retaining their own distinct personalities.

Often, however, instead of blending, the marriage resembles the collision of two worlds traveling side by side in the same orbit, but separated by a gulf. A gulf always exists when just one person extends himself or herself fully to blend, while the other only partially and even reluctantly responds.

Blending only occurs when there is "disclosure"—the willingness to reveal yourself to your mate. Too often (and this will probably be labeled as men bashing!) men are "reluctant revealers" who tend to withhold their feelings.

MEN AND EMOTIONAL EVASION

The more a wife tries to find out who her husband really is rather than who he publicly appears to be, the more he tends to withdraw. Her probing into feelings he doesn't want to share may provoke him into becoming an "emotional evader."

The reluctant and emotionally erosive disclosure pattern typical of most men intensifies when discussion moves from the safer topics of tastes, interests, attitudes and opinions to the unsafe subjects of feelings, money and work. These unsafe subjects are too personal for most men because they expose their private identities.

A woman learns to draw conclusions based not upon verbal communication but on behaviors she must interpret. She makes these deductions in an attempt to get closer to her husband. Her conclusions are then presented to the man as an invitation to talk about it. Usually, however, the request to elaborate is rejected. When a man does not want to talk, he often responds with shrugs or statements indicating the issues are inconsequential, temporary, within his control or based on circumstances. Phrases he commonly uses to avoid communication are:

"I can handle it."

"It's no big deal."

"Talk about it? Why? That won't help."

"It's nothing for you to be concerned over."

"I'll get through it okay."

"It'll work out."[1]

Varying degrees of this destructive communication pattern may be seen in many marriage relationships. Frankly, it is no way to live. Deadlocks and distance in marriage are a prelude to disaster. Every marriage needs a warning: DO NOT TRY TO OPERATE WITHOUT DISCLOSURE. Emotional intimacy in marriage is built through sharing openly!

Three Steps to Emotional Disclosure
Can anything be done? Yes.

First, the wife must provide a safe environment so her husband can overcome his reluctance to share.

Second, she needs to discover exactly what is making him so reluctant to share. This can be done through careful questioning.[2]

Finally, men must decide to risk, learn to share and fulfill the original creative intent of their potential for relationship.

QUESTIONS ABOUT MEN'S QUESTIONS

We conducted two major surveys concerning men's issues to

discover what men are reluctant to discuss. The first survey conducted in 1992 was sent to more than 700 professional counselors, ministers, lay counselors and social workers. The survey question was, "What are the five most frequent questions or issues that men ask in counseling?" We were amazed to receive more than 700 responses.

Included in those 700 responses were more than 3,500 questions that men ask. Of course, each question reflected the same questions most of the other men asked again and again. Each was carefully considered, and only the most frequently asked questions were selected for this book.

The issues raised by some men who seek counseling reveal a sense of desperation. Their many attempts to resolve their problems have resulted in a futile dead end. They realize they need help. Other counselees seek help during the early stages of their concerns before reaching the desperation stage. Depending on where you are in your relational development, you may find yourself identifying with some of these questions as well as the questions derived from our second survey.

The second survey was a self-report presented in numerous conference settings and churches throughout the country. Four questions were asked:

1. What subject(s) do you think men hesitate most in bringing up or discussing with women?
2. What is it that you think women do not really understand about men?
3. What is the greatest inner struggle that men deal with, which women either do not know about or understand?
4. What one thing would you like your wife to do that would indicate to you that she understands and accepts what you deal with in your daily life?

The men were asked to give detailed responses; however, even with the anonymity of the survey many were reluctant to complete the forms. The responses that did come in, however, were invaluable. The men who responded represented all ages from various churches throughout the nation.

If you are a man, what would your response be to the first question: What subjects do you hesitate most to discuss with women? If you are a woman, how would the man in your life answer this question?

The selection of responses to this question was arranged into four categories and will be integrated into various chapters throughout this book.

Category 1
The first category of responses to the question, "What subjects do you hesitate most to discuss with women?" focused on projects, the past, change, appreciation, personal relationships, conflict, vulnerability (weakness or insecurity) and what women want. The answers were repeated consistently by those who responded. The following responses are gleaned from the second survey:

> I don't think most men like discussing subjects that add on to their "Honey Do" lists. We feel busy enough. I watch the ex-contractor neighbor walk away briskly as we all stand in the street talking about our house projects, when his wife changes the subject to her wish for a remodeled kitchen! I know I turn off the switch in my head when I have "HER" list because I'd rather be tinkering on my projects. That's honest. I also don't think men like to hear or see commercials about the gals' period time of the month. We freak out. If a woman talks about this in serious terms, we don't want to know the details.

> Deep, personal feelings that perhaps we ourselves are afraid of or don't understand.

> Job issues or other problems where we've had a "history" of issues; for example, hard time keeping a job.

> Concerns or issues that never were solved or

73

dealt with, with our own mothers, that now come up in various ways in our marriages. For example, how can I give to someone else emotionally what I myself never got? How can I explain this?

Change. In general it is difficult to discuss changing certain aspects of our lives because of the uncertainty the changes might bring or require. I know that sounds like a lack of faith, but I also know that the Lord has put us where we are for a reason and that He has given us the ability to make decisions and process things.

    a. Attempted projects that are failing.
    b. Negative financial situations.
    c. Details about people and events.

The need to be appreciated.

Deep needs or insecurities, inadequacies, temptations

The wife's feelings about the state of her relationship and where it needs improvement.

I think the subjects men most hesitate to bring up with women are sex and finances. Because they provoke such personal feelings and attitudes, they are very sensitive subjects. Both men and women have such innate differences of approach to each of these subjects that conflict is very probable. That possibility makes men hesitate bringing up the subjects. If we were attentive to discussing these and other difficult subjects when things are good in these areas and not just at times when things are bad, maybe it wouldn't be so difficult to discuss them with women.

Personal relationships. I do not like to pry into

the personal relationships of others. When a conversation heads in this direction, I quickly resort to what God has to say...who can argue?

Potential conflict (this would be different for each couple); insecurities or areas of perceived failure (problems at work, lack of spiritual growth or plateaus); things that make us different. In today's world, men experience pressure to conform to the way women want us to be.

Issues or sins from the past that cause fear because of embarrassment or rejection. For example: sexual behavior (pornography, homosexuality) and criminal acts (theft, assault). Lingering feelings regarding these things, and persistent desires for them. Feelings about work.

If you talk about any other women, they had better be ugly. My wife seems to want to compare, rate and know what you think and why if the topic comes up.

In short, their own vulnerabilities. In our society men are supposed to be strong, self-sufficient "Clint Eastwood" types. Men impose this on themselves. It is difficult for men to show weakness or vulnerability, especially to women.

Our weaknesses, struggles, sex, relationships, finances, business loans and private schooling, lust.

Weakness in two areas: character and discipline.

A man's reputation is important to him. So when character issues come up, he translates them to be attacks on his reputation, when in reality it is dealing with an inner quality.

My wife and I share *everything* and are *very*
open—we have a great marriage—*only very slight
hesitation* regarding the intimacy of our sex life.
Except for the actual "act," we never discuss sex,
but I suppose it is *not* that important.

Any performance or character attribute that
makes them feel less than perfect. Especially their
own sexuality and feelings of job-related inadequacy.

How they feel about being a man and how
hard it is for men to open up to themselves much
less to other men or to women. Women are too
quick to tell men how they feel rather than help-
ing them get in touch with themselves and their
emotions.

Insecurity and that they don't have it all together; they are not perfect; they need help; they need
a woman to come along side of them and make life
successful. That plays itself out in needing public
affirmation and it also plays itself out in needing
sex. It may come across to women more like,
"Hey, I need sex" more than "I need you to know
that I'm insecure in this area."

Their leadership roles in the family. In today's
society the man's role is unrecognizable. We as
Christian men are told what our roles are to be bib-
lically. But when we take a stand *sometimes* we are
pegged as chauvinists, unfortunately, even from
Christian women!

My answer would be twofold. First, my wife
has experienced some abuse and does not feel
open about our sexuality. In order to protect her I
have to approach how I feel very carefully. I don't
want her to feel pressure, but at times she does.

Secondly, my own moments of anger. When she is angry she expresses HERSELF FREELY but I tend to hold back. I would like more FREEDOM to express my frustrations or anger.

True heartfelt problems, because a woman's emotional makeup many times does not enable her to just *listen*. She starts talking and makes it worse.

Their expectations of "who" and "what" they want their wives to be. Especially if a man's wife is not meeting his expectations; it is really tough to discuss. And, it is even more difficult to discuss when the man doesn't even have a clear picture of those expectations himself. Sometimes I think my expectations are too high or unrealistic, so if I don't have a handle on them in my own mind, how can I discuss them with my wife?

77

The previous comments confirm that men hesitate to be emotionally open with their wives because of the uncertainty of the outcome. They feel fear about potential conflict, discomfort about being personal, embarrassment, rejection, shame about admitting weakness, inability to know how to respond and concern about hurting their partners.

Each reason for being hesitant is legitimate; however, it is also insufficient to justify silence and prolong the lack of communication in relationships. The stressful residual effects of bottling up emotions can be enormous.

Category 2

The second category of responses centered on parenting, fears, aging and finances. The following are the men's self-reported responses:

Quality of fathering. Asking questions such as, "How am I doing as a husband?" or, "How are we doing as a couple?"

Their fears, namely financial and work related. Also their abilities to be good fathers and husbands. They also seem to question their relationship skills and appear hesitant to bring this up around women.

Financial problems and mistakes (bounced check!). Personal sexual desires/needs (different style or position for sex).

Masculine and feminine role issues. Men fear being accused of being sexist.

Discipline of children is a touchy subject because women have pre-conceived ideas that make it hard to act as priests of the home.

Finance, sex, things I would like to see my wife do (i.e., exercise and improve diet, dress better and other improvements related to house and home).

Finances, children, shortcomings, fears of succeeding and not ultimately providing them with emotional support.

Getting older, reaching lifetime goals, mortality.

Fear. Attraction to other women. Pressure of supporting the family. Frustration of unfulfilled desires and dreams.

Finances is a tough subject because it usually leads to one of us coming across as accusing the other of unnecessary spending.

Feelings and Finances

What questions and issues concern men most about finances? We referred to the survey based upon the responses of men in counseling from the 700 counselors for our answers.

Questions from 40 categories were compiled. Finances were near the top of the list, ranking ninth in frequency. Can you identify with any of their questions?

- Can't she spend less on herself and the kids? Can't she work part-time and help with these bills?
- How can I advance my career and provide more money for my family?
- How can I be financially responsible and still do what I want?
- How can I deal with a wife whose spending is out of control?
- How can I tithe and pay all of the bills?
- How do I establish a budget?
- How do I get control of my spending and still give my family the things they need?
- How do I handle the problem of managing money when it is "her money" or "my money," not "ours"?
- I feel tremendous financial pressure. How can I cope?
- I may be unemployed soon. How do I support my family?
- My wife and I fight over finances—I want to pay the bills, she "needs" to buy stuff. What's the solution?
- My wife gets so frantic about money. How can I help her to grow in faith and stop worrying so much?

Feelings About Communication

Another group of questions reflect men's concerns about communication—with their wives and with others:

- Why do I have trouble showing and telling my family how I really feel?
- How do I communicate more effectively with my adolescent children?
- I can't open up to her. In my family we didn't show our feelings. What can I do?

- She won't hear me out—so I clam up.
- We keep going over the same ground. How many times do I have to reconquer the same territory?
- What should I say?
- When I choose to be honest about my feelings, why do I feel so weak and misunderstood?
- When I start sharing my feelings (fears and anger) it only triggers her feelings. Then I, in turn, stop sharing. I feel that there's no place for me to share my feelings.
- Why am I so afraid to tell others how I feel or what I need? Why don't I trust?
- How can I tell the truth when it might come back on me?
- Why can't I communicate with women? or other men?
- Why can't she see where I'm coming from?
- Why can't we talk without things getting out of hand?
- Why do I have to tell her what I feel and have to ask for what I need?
- Why do women always expect men to talk about their feelings?
- Why do women always want to talk?
- Why should I open up? (She'd just get mad if I told her what I think the problem is.)

Feelings About Feelings

Feelings and emotions in addition to the man-woman relationship pose endless struggles for men. Hear what men are saying about these topics:

> Personal fears and "perceived inadequacies." Any subject that will trigger my wife's insecurities, resulting in hours of defensive discussion to alleviate her fears.

> Men's feelings of insecurity, incompleteness, inadequacy, loss of control of family and situa-

tions, lack of self-confidence and relating past mistakes. I personally did not want to share the above with my wife until this learning experience—I will share now!

Feelings of inferiority, depression, anxieties, etc. Men see it as weakness and I think we feel women will view it likewise. As Thoreau said, "Most men lead lives of quiet desperation."

It is very difficult for men to talk about sexual desires, personal feelings and emotions. I am very analytical. Black and white. On and off.

Their hidden fears of being rejected in *feelings* dealing with spouse or friends. Sometimes it is hard to drop that "PRIVATE WALL" around those "feelings."

Emotions. Also they won't talk a lot about family brokenness. They will hesitate to speak of loneliness, sadness or pain. Many times the only thing that will break them loose is when the wife is ready to walk out.

Emotional, feeling-oriented issues. Also issues dealing with failure since culturally men are to be strong and in control.

For me, the subjects hardest to discuss with my wife are my fears and insecurities and my sense of inadequacy I often experience. Another subject that is difficult to discuss is my struggle with lust, though I think my difficulty in discussing it is also rooted in fear: fear of rejection, fear of hurting her, fear of facing my own corruption.

Their spiritual relationship with God. Their shortcomings.

The inner struggle of juggling work, social life, family life and spiritual life. Knowing when and how to talk sensitively with my wife about my feelings and thoughts.

Anything that concerns a man's innermost thoughts and feelings. Two that come to mind right away are past failures (job, relationship, etc.) and desires concerning sex and intimacy.

Fears of life: failure, inferiority, losing one's job, impotence.

We also referred to the first survey based upon the counseling responses to discover specific questions related to men's feelings.

- How can I get in touch with and express my feelings without feeling inferior or that I am not in control?
- How can I share my feelings and still maintain my masculinity?
- How do I deal with feelings that have been denied?
- If I give up drinking, smoking, burying myself in work and let myself feel, could I handle it?
- Isn't it unreasonable for my wife to expect me to talk so much about emotions?
- Why am I so set on not expressing or showing my real emotions even though I'm hurting so much on the inside?
- Why do I numb out?
- Why is it so hard for me to talk about feelings or to cry?

If you are a man, are these questions speaking for you? With which ones do you identify? What would you add?

If you are a woman, what surprises you about these questions? Are some of these statements reflective of the man in your life? What can you do to encourage more sharing? One man sums it up:

> I'll tell you what would help me share more with
> my wife. For me to open up with her, there has to
> be no risk. I can be honest but I don't want to be
> hassled. I don't want to be judged for what I share
> and I want to share for as long as I want—and then
> have the freedom to quit when I need to.

No risk! No risk! Risk is a big factor in the man-woman
relationship. Men are risk takers in many other areas of life,
but only in areas where they can fall back on resources.
Sharing feelings presents a risk with a bottomless abyss waiting for us if we slip. Other men have expressed what hinders
them from sharing and what would help them:

> My wife is an expert on what is a "feeling" and
> what isn't a "feeling." I have tried to tell her what
> is going on inside of me and she tells me, "But
> that's not a feeling." Where is this book she uses to
> tell herself what is a feeling and what isn't? I feel
> like giving up if I'm never going to get it right.

> Yeah, I shared my feelings. And you know
> what happened? I opened up about work and my
> frustrations and she claimed I just wanted sympa-
> thy and attention. I tried to show her some love
> and attention and she said, "You must want some-
> thing, like sex. You've got some other motive in
> mind." I try to be what she wants and I get criti-
> cized because my motives are suspect.

> My wife tells me what I ought to be feeling. If
> she feels a certain way, I should feel the same way.
> If we watch a gripping movie, she wants me to feel
> what she feels. When she cries at church, she says,
> "But didn't you feel the same way? How could
> you not feel that way about what was shared?"
> Women's feelings are not the only right feelings,
> and if I have to feel the same way, it will never
> work. Can't two people in the same situation feel

differently and with a different intensity—and even express it differently?

It is important first to define the issues clearly. I don't think women do this very well. They latch on to the first thing that comes to mind and get totally emotionally involved in it. The next thing you know, you are arguing about everything under the sun, and no one is happy. I believe in a clear definition of the problem at the outset. If she can tell me exactly what is bothering her, we can deal with it logically. If she can't do that, then there is no sense even talking about it.

She expects me to have all these reactions right at my fingertips and be able to call them up on the spot. Well, I can't do that. I don't operate the way she does. *I need a little more time to think things through.* I don't want to say something I'm going to regret later on. Somehow she has the idea that wanting time to think is not being open and honest with her. That is ridiculous! I'm not trying to hide anything, I'm just trying to be sure in my own mind before I talk to her about it. What is wrong with that?

Men are just more rational than women. We prefer to deal with things in a thoughtful, rational way. Women are emotional, and that's the way they want men to deal with things. Just because a man prefers to discuss things logically doesn't mean he is any less involved than a woman who wears her emotions on her sleeve

Many men choke when it comes to sharing tender, caring feelings with others. They are not cruel, insensitive, noncaring people; they merely find it impossible to communicate their inner reservoirs of emotional expression.

I have talked with such men. I remember one in particular

who said, "I was so proud of my wife the other day. She has been taking some art lessons and finished her painting. It was displayed in the window of the artist's studio and two people wanted to buy it for an incredible amount of money! I don't know that much about art, but I thought it was great and was really feeling good about her success."

I replied, "That's great. How much of what you just shared with me did you tell her?"

He looked at me and said, "Well, I'm sure she knows how proud I am of her."

I replied, "How? How would she know that? Did you tell her what you told me? Did you tell her you were proud of her? Did you tell her you were feeling good about her success? Did you tell her you thought her art was great?"

He waited pensively, then looked up at me and said, "No, I guess I didn't. It would make a difference wouldn't it?"

I replied, "Yes, it could change her perception of you to that of a caring person if you would let her in on those feelings."

85

How Men Can Learn to Express Their Feelings

What can a man do who has never learned to share his feelings? Several steps can make a difference.

First, never compare yourself with a woman's ability. Comparison may keep you from trying. You listen to women share and think, *Forget it, I couldn't share like that, nor do I want to!* No one is suggesting that you share the way a woman does, but you can develop the untapped potential for expressing your unmasked feelings and developing intimacy.

Second, realize that becoming aware of and sharing your feelings offers you a multitude of life-changing benefits. It brings you closer to God's intended plan for your life. As a result, you will relate significantly better to a wider range of people, including feelings-oriented men and women. More people will listen to you and respond to you. Psychologically and physically you will be giving your wife one of the most desired gifts you could ever give her—real intimacy! And you will set a great role model for your children.

Third, listen to how others describe and share their feelings. Learn from them. Make a list of feeling words and memorize them. Expand other areas of your vocabulary as well, and use these new terms in sentences within your mind until you become comfortable with them. Some men I know have practiced out loud to accustom themselves to hearing the spoken words. (See the table at the end of the chapter for a list of "feeling" words.)

Fourth, learn to use word pictures to describe what is going on inside of you. Instead of just saying "I had a hard day," you could describe your day like this: "At times today it was so rough and frustrating, I felt like I was trying to push an elephant out of the way and finally it sat on me!" Or, "At one point today, it seemed like it was raining on everything I tried. I was really discouraged."

Fifth, try writing out what is going on inside of you. If you have a habit of saying "I think," you could change it to "I feel" or "I felt" or "my inner reaction was." Practice, pray and believe that God can work in your emotional life.

Sixth, let your wife know that one of your goals is to learn to share your feelings, and that you need her help and support. The following suggestions will alleviate misunderstanding and help to enlist the support you need:

1. Explain that it will be difficult for you, and that it would be helpful to you if she recognized your progress.
2. Let her know that sometimes the way you share may not seem clear and may differ from the way she would share in response to the same experience. Let her know that you want to understand. Tell her it would be best if she just asked a simple clarifying question rather than giving you correction.
3. Give yourself permission to process your thoughts. There will be times when you need first to think through what you are feeling to access your emotions. If there is silence, don't fill it in with words or questions.
4. Ask for understanding and grace. Tell her that

when feelings are shared, you don't want to hear judgments or criticisms.

5. Ask for confidentiality when personal feelings are shared. Let her know that you would prefer that these not be shared with others.

6. State clearly what you want. If you don't want to *discuss* your feelings but simply *state* them, let your wife know. If you don't want to talk about your feelings at the time or even later, let her know that, too. She is not a mind reader.

7. When your wife wants to discuss her feelings, find a time that is agreeable for both of you. Turn off the TV, don't answer the phone, lock up the kids, put down the newspaper, put the dog in the refrigerator—and now that I've got your attention—look at her, listen, reflect her feelings by asking questions and clarifying what you heard, don't take what she says as a personal attack and don't try to fix her.

How Women Can Express Their Feelings to Men

What is the best way for a woman to express her emotions to her husband—especially if he has difficulty coping with feelings?

Plan ahead and practice whenever possible. Share your feelings in small increments (piecemeal); don't dump them all at once. Emotional overloading tends to short-circuit and overwhelm men.

Ask a man, "What is your reaction?" rather than, "What are you feeling?"

Think of communicating with a man as speaking your native language to someone from another culture. I have learned to do this with my Asian students, and they appreciate it.

Two wives shared with me how they helped their husbands with the communication process.

One said, "Honey, when I share my feelings with you it's difficult for me to edit. I will probably talk too much and dump a load of emotions all over you. I just want you to know this in advance. You don't have to catch them all, just listen. If you want, I can repeat."

The other wife told her husband, "I appreciate you for sitting and listening to all this stuff. I'm not sure about all I just said. You probably feel the same way. Let's not talk now, but think about it and then sort through everything later. What do you think?" Both of these wives made it easier for their husbands.

Keep in mind several cautions when a man expresses his feelings (which most women count as a gift).

Never, but never, interrupt. I remember the first occasion I shared with my wife, Joyce, about the times when I had been depressed. I sat at the dining area table and Joyce stood 30 feet away with her back to me washing the dishes. When I started sharing, she stopped what she was doing, came over, sat down and listened. Never once did she interrupt or make a value judgment on what I was sharing. I felt safe.

Interruptions cause men to retreat and think, *Why bother sharing?* Sharing feelings takes more effort, energy and concentration for men than it does for women. Men need to stay focused on one thing at a time. Interruptions throw men off course; and because men are goal conscious, they like to stay on course and complete the process.

Distractions make it difficult for men to sort through the time-consuming process of interpreting their emotions. Many men are not emotionally articulate, because they lack language skills in this area. When women are patient and accept this lack, it helps us to talk more.[3]

A wife shared with me a commitment note she gave her husband. She said it produced the change in her husband she had wanted for years. The note read, "Since sharing your emotions with me is such a cherished experience and so vital to a wonderful sexual relationship, I commit myself to you to respond in the following manner: When you share, you can count on me to listen, not expect you to describe your feelings exactly as I do, not interrupt, nor make value judgments. And finally, if we do enter into a discussion, I will limit my participation to 15 minutes."

Two days later she received a dozen roses and a note that said, "Thank you," and then, "My commitment when you share is 'ditto.' I won't try to solve the problem unless you ask me to!"

THERE IS HOPE!

It is possible for men to become more open. One husband had this to say:

> I simply would not be the way I am today if my wife had not stood by me every step of the way. It was still hard to set aside years of socialization and actually become a new, loving man. Knowing that I had someone by my side helped me get over the rough spots, too. Anybody who thinks there won't be any is fooling himself. To my way of thinking, anybody who tries to go it alone is just a fool. It simply can't be done. As much as a man likes to think he can do things on his own, when it comes to being more loving, a man has to have help. There are just too many things that can go wrong.[4]

And another:

> One of the first things I had to learn was to shut off thinking. There's such a difference between feeling and thinking. Thinking is what we men are good at; the rational, logical approach is how we go at things. When a problem comes up, my first response used to be, "What makes sense here?" Now I'm trying to hold off on what makes sense and ask instead, "What do I sense here?" There's a big difference.[5]

Men can change; however, they usually don't change by choosing to *be* different. A crucial point for women to remember is that men are task oriented, not feeling oriented. They change by deciding to *behave* differently. They need objective

89

awareness, not a feeling, for the change to occur. When a man can think, *There is a problem out there. I can do something different to fix it,* change is on the horizon. When a man thinks, *I am the problem; I am at fault,* change is nowhere in sight.[6]

Men do change. Let me repeat that. We do change! Yes, it's possible, but we are only interested in changing, as Dr. John Gray suggests, when we feel appreciated and accepted. When we realize we can do something to achieve the desired result, we accept the challenge and we feel motivated to change.[7]

The following is a sampling of eight feeling words, including amplification and related terms. Practice using these words when conversing with others to enhance your ability to describe your feelings.

FEELING WORDS

Hate	*Fear*	*Anger*	*Happiness*
1. dislike	1. frightened	1. sore	1. joyful
2. bitter	2. terror	2. offended	2. enthusiastic
3. hateful	3. anxious	3. mad	3. merry
4. odious	4. misgivings	4. resentful	4. blessed
5. detest	5. concerned	5. wrathful	5. fortunate
6. spiteful	6. harassed	6. hostile	6. pleased
7. aversion	7. dread	7. displeased	7. glad
8. despise	8. alarm	8. injured	8. satisfied
9. loathe	9. apprehensive	9. vexed	9. contented
10. abominate	10. worry	10. torment	10. delighted

Love	*Disappointment*	*Sadness*	*Confusion*
1. affection	1. disturbed	1. depressed	1. mixed up
2. loving	2. unhappy	2. grief	2. doubtful
3. amorous	3. dissatisfied	3. dejected	3. disorder
4. likable	4. frustrated	4. torment	4. bewildered
5. tenderness	5. deluded	5. anguish	5. confounded
6. devotion	6. defeated	6. sorrow	6. disarray
7. attachment	7. hurt	7. unhappy	7. jumble
8. fondness	8. failure	8. gloomy	8. uncertain
9. passion	9. rejection	9. melancholy	9. perplexed
10. endearing	10. thwarted	10. mournful	10. embarrassed

REFLECTING ON THIS CHAPTER

1. As a wife, have you learned how to draw out your husband's feelings even if he is reluctant to express them?
2. As a male, how could your wife make it easier for you to express your feelings more freely?
3. What are some negatives that can threaten a relationship if one partner evades "disclosure" or has difficulty expressing true feelings?
4. As youths, did you and your spouse learn to deal with feelings in radically different ways? Do you see these patterns affecting your marriage?
5. Are specific topics or areas harder for you to talk about than others? If so, why?
6. Can you discuss your feelings better at certain times than you can at other times? Does your spouse know this?

Notes

1. Michael E. McGill, Ph.D., *The McGill Report on Male Intimacy* (New York: HarperCollins, 1986), pp. 38-46.
2. For assistance with this, see the resources listed in notes 4 and 5.
3. Barbara De Angelus, *Secrets About Men Every Woman Should Know* (New York: Delacote Press, 1990), pp. 234-242, adapted.
4. Michael McGill, *The McGill Report on Male Intimacy* (San Francisco: HarperCollins, 1985), p. 269, adapted.
5. Ibid., p. 276, adapted.
6. H. Norman Wright and Gary Oliver, *How To Change Your Spouse* (Ann Arbor: Servant Publications, 1994), pp. 231ff., adapted.
7. John Gray, *Men, Women & Relationships* (Hillsboro, Oreg., Beyond Words Publishing, 1990), pp. 116, adapted.

7

MEN AND THEIR FEELINGS ABOUT SEX

Men are sexual. There is no getting around that fact. As one wife observed, "When it comes to sex, a man's 'on' button is never off."

Men do think about sex more than women. They think about it, dream about it and daydream about it more than many people realize. From several times an hour to several times a day sexual thoughts bombard the male mind, depending, of course, on the individual man.

Many typical male characteristics find their expression through sex. The male performance drive finds an outlet in the sexual relationship. Men want to perform well sexually. They greatly fear the inability to do so. Many men use their sexual abilities to prove their manhood, and some are quite open about their conquests.

In response to our first survey question, "What subjects do you think men hesitate most in bringing up or discussing with women?" sex was at the top of the list.

GENDER DIFFERENCES
IN SEXUALITY

Let's look at some of the sexual differences between men and women.

Sex has different meaning for men than for women in love relationships. Most women give sex to achieve emotional closeness; however, men tend to view being close as sex.

Women view sex as one way of being close, but too many men view it as the only way to be close.

Tenderness, touching, talking and sex go together for a woman. Many men think sex is sufficient, especially if they do not know how to achieve intimacy in other ways. It is easy for men to substitute sex for sharing.

Sex is an expression of emotion; however, for many men it often serves as a substitute for emotion. A wife expressed her feelings about sex with her husband in the following words:

> To me being close means sharing and talking. He thinks being close is having sex. Maybe that is the difference in the way we love. When he's upset or mad or insecure, he wants sex. I guess it reassures him. I wish he would talk about the feelings. When I get home from work and I'm wound up with a lot of baggage, I want to talk about it. When he comes home that way, he doesn't want to talk, he wants sex. When I'm sad, what I need is a shoulder to cry on and someone to hear me out. When he's sad, he wants to be seduced out of his feelings.

One husband said:

> Sure, sex means many things to me. Sometimes I want sex with my wife because I feel romantic and want to be loving and close. Other times I just want the release or diversion. I don't need to talk all the time about it. I wish she could understand that. It can't always be romantic.

Too many men believe that sex can replace other kinds of communication in a relationship. They think sex will suffice for sharing their personal and private selves. It is as though a husband says to his wife, "You ought to know I love you because I make love to you."

For women, sex is only one means of intimacy among many—and not always the best one. For many men, sex is the only expression of intimacy. The sexual act for most women is gradually built. As an older book title by Kevin Leman put it, *Sex Begins in the Kitchen.*

Men tend to condense intimacy into the sex act. When they do not have that outlet, they can become frustrated and upset. Why? Because they are cut off from the only source of closeness they know. Men are interested in closeness and intimacy, but they define and express it differently than women do. Men and women need to talk, listen and understand each other's sexual viewpoints.

SEX AND COMMUNICATION

Men hesitate discussing sex with their wives because they fear making fools of themselves. They are supposed to be the strong, tough ones; therefore, they are afraid to make themselves vulnerable. Men are supposed to know all about sex.

In a survey of men attending Promise Keeper events, 57 percent said they were afraid to confide their sexual thoughts to others.[1]

Why should we be surprised that men don't really open up and talk in depth about sex? It is a very private area, and it means running a risk.[2]

SURVEYS OF
MEN AND SEXUALITY

"The Hart Report," a study of men and sex in the '90s conducted by Dr. Archibald Hart, provides some accurate and informative data based upon a sample of sexually conservative men, including many ministers. The report includes the results of more than 600 surveys as well as counseling feedback gleaned from men during a 25-year period. The vast majority of those involved in Dr. Hart's research were from the 30 to 50 age group.

What was discovered in the report?

> For one thing, most men do not have very many others to talk to about sex. About 65 percent said their spouse or partner was the only one they could discuss it with. 20 percent said they had friends they talked to about it but 25 percent said there was no one to talk to. And probably for those who talked with their wives there were limits to what they could or would share.[3]

The following major concerns expressed in Dr. Hart's research were consistent with our own studies:

> Men were concerned about being oversexed. Their questions usually had more to do with the learned ways of expressing sexuality than the basics of sexual arousal. A second question concerned being undersexed. The final one which our survey reflected so much was "How can I control my sex drive?"[4]

A sampling follows from our own survey of responses that answer the question: What are men hesitant to bring up and discuss with women?

> Sexuality. Not simply the physical and erotic aspects, but also the visual aspect. I always try to look good for my wife. I shave more and dress better for her than for work. I brush my teeth and comb my hair... etc. But I'm not convinced she is reciprocating, or at least I may not be noticing if she is. But I can't very well say, "Please wear eye makeup," or "put on earrings," etc. She has never owned any earrings. I like the natural look and she is attractive, but sometimes I'd like a little special effort.

Sex—we do it, but we don't discuss it in depth. Maybe it's a pride thing with men. We don't discuss it because we men might not be meeting our mate's needs. We discuss when, but rarely why or how.

Negative aspects of your spouse's physical appearance or character. Her weak points.

Sexual fantasies, thoughts and desires. It may make the wife feel that she does not satisfy her husband. It may hurt her feelings and women don't usually forget.

Sexual thoughts, desires, fantasies—because a man's mind seems to be more active in this area. We are aroused merely by visual stimulus and/or thoughts—it remains a tough subject to discuss with women/wives.

Sex—men may think they are imposing on women. They may be tired of being rejected. Things men want to try sexually that are not accepted by their partners.

Their sex lives. I have a very passive partner in bed and this causes a less than satisfying sexual experience for me. I have approached the subject several times and have received very negative responses.

A few issues come to mind here. Physical desires within our relationship. When it's good it's GREAT, however, with the demands of our daily lives, finding the right time presents challenges.

I never bring up discussions about the struggles I have with sexual fantasies. As a man, seeing a beautiful woman walk by can bring many thoughts and really get the mind going. I don't think she would understand if we discussed this.

That I can be sexually attracted to other women. I am afraid it will hurt her self-image.

Sex. I will not openly discuss sex or pornography with my wife or other women. I even hesitate to discuss sex with my wife. She immediately becomes defensive and comments "That is all you ever think about." Maybe she is right, but I believe we, as a couple, should have a good understanding of the other's expectations and desires.

The wife's overweight. The wife's appearance. Sexual problems on the man's part, e.g., lust, temptation, masturbation, pornography. The wife's sexual response.

Sex and romance.

Sex and finances.

Sex—what they really want in bed and how to give pleasure.

The need for intimacy, the specifics about how to be loved and give love.

Sexual desires with wives, emotions, their inadequacies, fears.

Personal lust struggles.

The questions about sex that men have brought to counseling are consistent and repetitive. A few of these repetitive questions follow.

- Can I ever be cured of my sexual temptations?

- Can you help me with my problem with pornography, sexual frustration, fantasies, etc.?
- How can I control my lust?
- How can I control my sexual desires and remain pure?
- How do I control my desire to look lustfully at other women?
- How can I control my thought life and my eyes?
- How do I deal with my obsessive sexual thoughts?
- I am attracted to other women and have sexual fantasies about them. Is this wrong? What can I do?
- Why did God give men such strong sex drives and women so little sex drive?
- Can you help me understand the difference between intimacy and sexuality? How can I get close and open to someone else (male or female) and not always be sexual?
- How do I deal with my fear of impotency?
- How do I handle my sexual dysfunction?
- How is intimacy different from sex?

99

WHAT DO MEN WANT FROM SEX?

Men do want more from sex than sex! They want "complete" relationships. Complete—meaning intimate—sexually, emotionally, spiritually and relationally. Men do hunger for intimacy, despite the fact that many substitute sex for sharing and emotion. Some, however, are able to connect with both.

Men who tend to confuse emotional needs for sexual needs and view intimacy as sex become frustrated, grumpy and upset when they don't have a sexual outlet. Sex is usually their only source of closeness.

Although men want sex, they are often unsure of what they want and how to obtain it. The problem is not insurmountable. Both men and women need to talk, listen and discuss their sexual needs. Many men feel more comfortable discussing sex in the darkness of the bedroom because the risk of intimate sharing is diminished there.

Approximately 150 men who participated in the Hart report were asked the question, "Do you feel that women understand men's sex drive?" The response was a strong 83 percent "no," which probably indicated a lack of sufficient sex in their own relationships.[5]

What do men want their wives to understand about their sexuality? That they are normal when it comes to sex. That an understanding of one another's needs must be recognized and that both partners must work toward mutual satisfaction.

Men want their wives to understand and accept the strength of their biological drives. The male sex drive is not a fault nor is it a mistake. God is the author of sex. Men want their wives to know that looking at other women does not mean they don't love their wives. A look of admiration is not a sign of straying.

Men want their wives to initiate lovemaking—at least part of the time. They get weary of being the pursuer, and they do appreciate some novelty.

At times men do not want sex, but they do want closeness. Often wives interpret every physical overture as a prelude to ending up in bed and sometimes for good reason. No one is a mind reader. It simplifies everything when you verbalize your intent and desire.[6]

EVER ON THEIR MINDS

How much do men think about sex? Is that a necessary question? Men see sex everywhere and in everything. Sexual thoughts flow in and out of men's minds all day long. Though men slow down their sexual thinking during their 40s and 50s, they still think about it several times a day. Sixteen percent of the conservative Christian men surveyed in the Hart report said they thought about it hourly.[7]

Men also tend to dream about sex three times as often as women, and their dreams rarely involve their own wives. Women object to the notion that the majority of men admit to fantasizing about other women for sexual stimulation. Fantasizing seems to be intriguing, and many men need some kind of fantasy (whether a real person or not) to become sexually aroused. With the appropriate person this may not be a problem, but no wife can compete with a fantasy. Two of the major problems with fantasy are its addictive nature and its tendency to lead to acting out—fulfilling the fantasy.[8]

Men think about sex more often than they like to admit. We think about it during the day, when we go to bed and when we wake up. Archibald Hart describes it well:

> Sure, the average man thinks of other things, like football and politics, but eventually all mental roads lead back to this one central fixation: Sex. There are times when the obsession fades and even vanishes. Give him a golf bag or a fishing trip. He'll forget about sex for a while. But sooner or later, like a smoldering fire, it will flare up again. Strong, urgent, forceful and impatient, the sex drive dominates the mind and body of every healthy male. Like it or not, that's the way it is.[9]

Another problem contributing to men's sexual struggles is the lack of understanding women show about the male sex drive. I do not mean to be diverting the blame or responsibility, but many women just don't understand this basic masculine need. Women are not as interested, obsessed or compulsive about it.

Some women are either vain about their looks or they simply enjoy tantalizing men. When they dress provocatively to attract one man, all men notice. Men are aroused by proximity, perfume and revealing clothing.

WHAT ABOUT SEXUAL FANTASIES?

The ability to think and imagine is a gift from God. It is part of being created human. Fantasy is useful for building a good marital sex life. It can also distort a relationship; but we should not fear fantasy. Men and women use their imaginations to enhance many areas of their lives.

First Peter says, "Therefore, prepare your minds for action;

be self-controlled....Do not conform to the evil desires you had when you lived in ignorance" (1:13,14, *NIV*). James states, "Each one is tempted when he is drawn away by his own desires and enticed. Then, when desire has conceived, it gives birth to sin" (1:14,15, *NKJV*).

Romans 12:2 talks about being "transformed by the renewing of your mind" (*NKJV*). Ephesians 4:23 says, "be renewed in the spirit of your mind" (*NKJV*).

These passages condone godly fantasy for building healthy sex lives in marriages. God ordained sex in marriage, therefore, sexual desire between mates is never wrong.

We have been given the power to control our imaginations. Our imaginations can eliminate thoughts that limit and distort wholesome sexuality and expand healthy thoughts and fantasies. Sexual desire is not wrong, but how we choose to use the desire can be.

Men and women build memory banks of erotic thoughts and behaviors. Pleasurable experiences, including sights, sounds and even smells (such as perfumes) are mentally recorded. Certain images become more erotically charged because they are linked to past sexual experiences.

FANTASY VERSUS LUST

Not all fantasy is lust. What exactly is lust? Jesus said:

> You have heard that it was said, "Do not commit adultery." But I tell you that anyone who looks at a woman lustfully has already committed adultery with her in his heart (Matt. 5:27,28).

Note that lust is not behavior—it is thinking. Lewis Smedes presents a helpful perspective about lust:

> There is no way of defining lust exactly; we must take Jesus seriously without pin-pointing the exact edge of the precipice. To "lust after" a person must have something to do with fanning desire into a flame of specific intent. And it probably has to do

with a narrow focus on another person's body.

It is foolish to identify every erotic feeling with lust. There is a sexual desire that feels like a lonely vacuum yearning to be filled, a longing for intimacy that broods within one's system. To identify this as lust is to brand every normal sexual need as adultery. Eros, the longing for personal fulfillment, must not be confused with lust, the untamed desire for another person's body. Nor is every feeling of attraction toward an exciting person the spark of lust. It would be odd indeed if the Creator put attractive people in the world and forbade us to notice them. But there is a difference between the awareness of someone's sexual body. Jesus did not choose to draw the line between them. But we should know that there is a difference, so that we will be neither too quick to feel guilt nor too careless with our feelings. Attraction can become captivity; and when we have become captives of the thought, we have begun to lust. When the sense of excitement conceives a plan to use a person, when attraction turns into scheme, we have crossed beyond erotic excitement into spiritual adultery. There need be no guilt when we have a sense of excitement and tension in the presence of a sexually stimulating person; but we also need to be alert to where that excitement can lead.[10]

It is difficult for a man today to be in public or even at home watching TV and not be sexually stimulated. A man responding to our survey said:

> I believe women do not understand the full impact of visual stimulation upon men. The television is a powerful source of visual stimulation, feeding the fantasies of most men who view the constant onslaught of fleshly temptations. I believe that wives would remove the televisions from their

homes if they fully understood how great a battle is waged by the TV for the minds and imaginations of their husbands. While men do not necessarily understand the negative impact of romantic novels upon their wives, so women seem to fail to identify the real impact of television (and most feature films as well).

The real problem is neglecting to control the eyes, the thoughts and the impulses. Neglect of self-control of these senses can destroy a relationship as well as a reputation. Neither the look of recognition nor the look of admiration is a problem; however, the look of lust is a problem. Fantasy distorts reality. It hides blemishes, enhances curves and blots out both physical and personality flaws. No real person can compete with a fantasy. The more flawless and unreal the sexual fantasy, the less satisfaction there can be with one's own spouse. Again Lewis Smedes suggests:

> What, then, of sexual fantasies? Almost everyone's imagination, at some time, produces sexually loaded fantasies. The more productive the imagination, the richer and more interesting the fantasies. Fantasy life can be treacherous. If we retreat too often into that world without risks, without demands, and without disappointments, it can become an escape from genuine encounters with real people. There is something tempting about fantasy life when real life is either dull or difficult. For people who habitually run away from reality that is less than perfect into the world where they can make everything turn out just as they wish, there is real danger. But the danger is not that of lusting so much as of unfairness to the real people who populate our real world of sexual relationships.[11]

The man quoted previously in response to our survey also shared this insight about men's thought lives:

Men are reluctant to identify their personal thought lives. Certainly our thoughts are flooded with competing messages both from God and from Satan. But when we decide to own the worldly thoughts from Satan we begin to nurture a sinful imagination. Many such imaginations are dangerous and even sinful, such as a focus on materialism, power and control. However, the most damaging to men seems to be the lustful imaginations. The imagination somehow drives us to fulfillment in the flesh, and I believe many men enter into affairs during their marriages because they have fed and nurtured lustful imaginations.

Scripture calls men and women alike to maintain pure thought lives and to make mature decisions when we are presented with sexual cues:

> Put to death, therefore, whatever belongs to your earthly nature: sexual immorality, impurity, lust, evil desires and greed, which is idolatry (Col. 3:5).

Any fantasy that diminishes your sexual interest, attraction and desire for your spouse is destructive to your marriage. In his insightful book *A Celebration of Sex,* Dr. Douglas Rosenau sums up the problem of lust in this manner:

> Destructive lust forgets that every person is special and three-dimensional with a body, soul, and spirit. Lust objectifies (makes a sexual object) a person and views the person as a detached body with only genitals and erotic appeal but no personality (soul). Lust can harm other people for personal sexual gratification because it has detached sex from a person and an intimate relationship.
>
> Harmful sexual thinking is immature and practices poor impulse control. You constantly focus on sexual stimuli in the environment; sex becomes a mental preoccupation. Sex invades your total life,

assuming too great an importance as you notice every little sexual cue. Sex can take on addictive proportions and sabotage a balanced life and caring relationships. Damaging sexual fantasy keeps looking at and obsessing about a person or sexual situation outside marriage. This "lusting after" sets up a person until the thinking begins to encourage the likelihood of sinful behaviors and infidelity. Sinful lust is often a detrimental pattern that comes out of and perpetuates a series of poor choices.

Injurious lust diminishes your attraction to your mate and can be insulting to your mate, who comes to feel inferior, embarrassed, or neglected. It detracts from your commitment to building a more exciting sex life with your partner. Sinful fantasy adulterates your enjoyment of your partner rather than enhances your sexual intimacy together.[12]

Do men and women differ in their lustful thoughts? Consider this suggestion from Charles Mylander, a minister from Southern California.

Often men and women experience different kinds of lust. Most men battle with impulsive lust based on physical attractiveness. Most women battle selective lust, desiring men whom they consider special. Men are led into sexual sin by lusting after women's bodies, most often beginning with the eye gates. Women are led into sexual sin by lusting after men's attentiveness, most often beginning with the ear gates.

Men fall into lust because of the enticement of physical pleasure. Lustful male fantasies prompt a physical stimulation that raises his voltage. Women fall into lust because of the enticement of emotional pleasure. Female lust most often takes the form of mental fantasy about romance with drama, a love affair with excitement or a triangle with intrigue. Lustful female fantasies cause emotional stimulation that likewise raises her voltage. Most men are first tempted by physical attraction while most women seem more vulnerable to emotional appeal. However, it is also true that some men find emotional attraction a powerful pull upon them and some women feel strong sexual urges from the visual sight of a well-built male. The Christian who finds both kinds of urges, physical and emotional, stimulated by the opposite sex must be doubly careful. When channeled in the right direction, this man or woman is often warm, attractive and caring—wonderful qualities in a Christian. Outside of Christ's control, however, this same person can fall easily into sexual immorality.[13]

FANTASY, SEX AND COMMITMENT

So what can a man do? We can use our sexual thoughts and responses in healthful ways. If you are a man you are going to admire, so admire. You are going to be sexually stimulated by what you see, so accept it.

Don't feed it. Don't dwell on it. Turn your sexual responses toward your wife. Fantasize about her. Don't be afraid of your thought life. Bring your fantasies into your married sexual relationship.

A single man will struggle with his sexuality—so will a single woman. There are no easy solutions. Victory requires commitment to Jesus Christ, obedience to His Word and restraint during times of sexual stimulation and frustration. Charles Mylander's *Running the Red Lights* (Regal) is the best resource I have found to help with this struggle.

The book *A Celebration of Sex* was mentioned previously in this chapter. If you would like to overcome your hesitation about discussing sexual issues with your wife and enrich your married sex life, read this book out loud together. Reading a book about sex aloud with your spouse may feel threatening, but the embarrassment can be overcome. It is a simple task, yet one that will benefit both of you. It has worked for many couples.

REFLECTING ON THIS CHAPTER

1. Do you view sex as primarily an *emotional* or a *physical* act?
2. Do you agree with the author that sometimes sex is used as a substitute for emotions?
3. What is the point of the book title, *Sex Begins in the Kitchen*? Do you agree with this statement?
4. What positive and negative values do you see in fantasizing about sex?
5. Do you think the increasing permissiveness about sex in the media is helpful or harmful to healthy marital relationships?

Notes

1. "Picture of a Promise Keeper," *New Man Magazine* (November 1995): 12.
2. Michael McCall, *The McGill Report on Male Intimacy* (New York: HarperCollins, 1985), pp. 58, 188-89, adapted.
3. Archibald Hart, *The Sexual Man* (Dallas: Word, Inc., 1984), p. 9.
4. Loc. cit.
5. Op. cit., p. 79, adapted.
6. Op. cit., pp. 78-81, adapted.
7. Op. cit., p. 61, adapted.
8. Loc. cit.
9. Op. cit., p. 5.
10. Lewis B. Smedes, *Sex For Christians* (Grand Rapids: William B. Eerdmans, 1976), pp. 210-11.
11. Loc. cit.
12. Douglas E. Rosenau, *A Celebration of Sex* (Nashville: Thomas Nelson, 1994), p. 94.
13. Charles Mylander, *Running the Red Lights* (Ventura, Calif.: Regal Books, 1986), pp. 53-54.

8

WHAT WOMEN DON'T UNDERSTAND ABOUT MEN: THE MEN SPEAK OUT

Several possible reasons exist for the tension between the sexes. It could be that women just do not understand some of the unique gender differences built into men by the Creator. Perhaps women do understand; but they refuse to accept the differences, so they campaign for change. In some cases, maybe they understand, but they have become passively tolerant. Possibly there are other possibilities!

Women have written numerous books and articles explaining their confusion and lack of understanding about men. Rarely, however, do men speak out in response to what women don't understand about them. So we asked men point blank, "What is it that you think women do not really understand about men?"

Listen with me to the answers we discovered. Imagine

that you are a participant at a conference about men's issues. The conference is attended by both men and women and the main session is about to begin.

Naturally, the conference has attracted many people—especially this session. The speaker has included the responses of more than 200 men to two questions: "What do you think women don't really understand about men?" and "What are men's greatest inner struggles?" The responses to these questions were very similar. Join me as the speaker begins:

Good evening ladies and gentlemen.

What I am going to share with you this evening are not my own thoughts and beliefs, but those that have come from the hearts, the minds and the lips of concerned men. They wished to remain anonymous and we will honor their privacy. But they have a dual message to share. They wish to be heard and understood by women, and they also want to encourage other men to speak out.

Allow their words to touch your hearts as these men speak for all of us. As much as possible, their own words and phrases are used. Here is what they said:

"We believe women don't fully understand that men are different from women. They appear to realize they are different from us, but they don't understand how different we are from them—and that it is good that we are different. The difference is not a negative. Let's keep in mind that God created us differently for a purpose. And it is good. We don't want to be like women.

"We know women want us to understand them. We are trying. But please cut us some slack and understand us, too; don't think all men are alike. We aren't.

"We men are competitive. We like it. We enjoy it. We also like "blazing new trails" and conquering new things like our ancestors did when they hammered out the new frontier during the founding of our country.

"Some of us go too far in this tendency and must be reminded of the need for balance. Keep in mind, however, that our competitiveness is needed to succeed for our families. Women often have difficulty accepting our "hunter" instincts. They don't understand our drive to win the race, accomplish the goal or complete the task. Sometimes we have a need to appear macho or masculine or whatever you want to call it. We want to appear strong and in charge—to ourselves, to others, especially to other men. Is this wrong?

"Our inner struggles are caused by our whole quests for balance. We strive to find a balance between 'fighting foes, providing, hunting, succeeding, etc.,' and 'being sensitive, caring, approachable, loving, etc.' These two concepts seem opposed. The world tells us to be tough, strong and in control; yet we want to be sensitive, available and nurturing.

"We also struggle with the balance between work and family. Family life takes time. Work life takes time. Both demand a lot of energy, sacrifice and determination. Both require personal resources. We men are stretched to the limit. We need to replenish our energies—our physical energies, mental energies and spiritual energies. Yet we struggle because we want to give 110 percent in every area of our lives.

"Women don't usually enjoy the same hobbies and interests as we do, but we want them to know that we need these outlets. They help us to *forget work*. And we need to forget it at times. When we play with the women in our lives, often we just want to play—not talk.

"We need to feel important. Whether it's work, sports, hobbies or family, we are searching for significance, approval and success. We have different drives and motivations, but most women don't recognize this. Our drive for success is often camouflaged with phrases like "it's no big deal"—but it is a big deal. And it is a very big deal to look good around our peers."

One man was quite candid with his thoughts about this subject:

"Most women know about men's egos, but they see our egos as character flaws. They fail to see that our egos can also be interpreted as positive qualities. Our egos compel us to lead, to serve and to protect women. We need to be valued and respected as family leaders and protectors.

"Most men are creators, builders. It can be anything from hot rods, barbecues, to room additions. We enjoy serving women in this way, but women need to explain what they want before we complete the project. It is disheartening and demotivating to have to make changes once the job is finished. We hate to hear, 'Oh, I wish we had done this instead' after the work is done.

"Most women don't understand that maturity is more than facial hair. We want women to be patient with us as we develop into men. We need guidance, mentoring and male friendships to grow and mature.

"We struggle with establishing identities. We can build relationships and we need male fellowship. But we define ourselves by what we do, not by our friendships. We want to know: Is this wrong? Is this a problem?

"We long to be appreciated for 'who we are,' especially at home. We want to experience unconditional love at home—not just performance-based love. We struggle with that all day long on the job. When we come home, we don't always want to hear how hard our wives have worked. We need to hear some loving compliments, not just complaints!

"Do women really understand how we feel about the responsibility for making ends meet? Their actions tells us they don't. We feel burdened to provide for the family whether our wives are employed or not. Many of us fear disappointing the family, and failing in our roles of protector, provider, father, family leader and spiritual head. Our self-worth, our ego and our identity are linked to both work and home. It often appears that we are not as interested in what goes on at home as we are with what happens at work. That may not always be the case—we may just be exhausted from work. It is frustrating for us not to have more time to give of ourselves at home."

One man expressed his greatest inner struggle this way:

"It is really tough being a man—at least the man that God expects me to be. There is a lot of internal pressure if I truly want to be a man of God—a leader in my home; a good, tender, loving and understanding husband; a gentle, wise, available and compassionate dad; a model and diligent worker (employee); and a trustworthy, listening and responsible friend. These are just a few of the responsibilities of a godly man in addition to being truly and wholly committed to loving, serving and obeying God."

Another man shared his struggle:

"I struggle to live up to not only life's, but also my wife's various expectations—you know, job position and success, good father, perfect husband. But actually, my greatest struggle is overcomimg the past without missing the 'now' and destroying the future. For example, I labor with not letting my 'non-feeling past' rob me of 'feeling today.' My grief over missed opportunities often destroys today's joy and tomorrow's possibilities. I feel like the 'weaker' vessel and at times I can barely handle the flood of emotion myself, let alone share it with another—especially a woman. Lord knows how she will react and use it against me. But, I am working on it, regardless of the consequences."

Other men said:

"We need to feel needed and know we are important at home. We are sensitive to not only *what* you say but also *how* you say it. Criticism shuts us down. We want our wives who are full-time homemakers and haven't worked in the competitive, chaotic work world outside of the home to understand that it is difficult and challenging for Christian men to interact and work under the constant influence of non-Christian attitudes all day."

One man summed it up for most of us when he said:

"We men live in fear of losing our income, our health and our morality. Our energies are spent keeping up our image of being good men, and being successful providers."

I see by the look on several faces in this audience that you would like nothing better than to interrupt these quotations of what men think. Let me remind you that this is part of the problem. Men need to be allowed to state their opinions without interruption or correction. Please give us this courtesy as I continue to quote from what men have said.

"Then we come to the big issue we're always taking hits about—emotions, feelings or whatever you call them. There is confusion here for both men and women. We are emotional beings. We are not as insensitive as we are stereotyped to be, but we have difficulty moving from the logical/linear side of the mind to the emotional—that is, if we are left-brained males. Not all of us are left brained either.

"We do need to be emotionally connected to the women in our lives. Women tend to label us as loners. It's not true for all of us—alone at times, yes, but not loners.

"There are a couple of reasons why men keep their deep feelings to themselves: one is to spare and shelter their wives from pain; the other is that we fear we will be told what to do or interrogated about what we have shared.

"It is painful to be referred to as 'typical males' and to always hear how incomplete and inadequate we are. We need to be accepted and appreciated for the way God created us."

Listen to what these three men said about feelings.
First:

> I would say many women don't understand the reality and depth of emotional pain men feel, especially when it is related to feelings of inadequacy imposed by society's markings of a real man— financial success, sexual potency, physical stature, competency, etc. I wonder if the average wife knows how much her husband needs her support, admiration and affirmation.

Second:

> My wife says things to me that hurt deeply. She says them in passing without much emotion or anger, just off the cuff. She seems to say them at times when discussion would be inappropriate (i.e., when other people are present). Finally when we do get time to talk, the hurt is less severe or I just let it pass. This is probably more my problem than hers.

And third:

> We struggle with emotions and stress. It seems that women, even those from the feminist groups, feel that they have all the stress. I don't know if they understand the gigantic responsibility we

face being God's umbrella of protection for our families in a world that has such great negative influence and unhealthy attractions. It is hard to keep all your ducks in a straight line at times.

Perhaps you relate to these three men. Perhaps you are bothered by what they have said. They're not alone. They're a voice for men past, present and future. Let me continue with some more responses from men:

"We need an abundance of emotional encouragement, positive strokes, touching and compliments just as women do. Those of us who are high achievers often mask our intense fears of failure and inferiority with our successes. We just don't like to admit it.

"Some of us feel crippled. Many of us won't ever fulfill the expectations of our wives. Can't we work out some level of compromise?

"Many of us would like to communicate with our wives as intimately as they communicate with their friends. But we find it difficult. Who will help us learn? We receive few offers—only complaints.

"Women say we are single-minded. We are. Single-mindedness helps us reach our goals. We have difficulty listening when we are concentrating on something else. We are accused of being purposely inattentive and made to feel guilty and even attacked for this. Why?

"We want women to understand that we need more time to process what is said to us than women do. When we feel pressured to be different, we may use anger as our protection—to get others to back off.

"Stereotypes limit us. Women are convinced that all men think about is power and sex, or sex and power! So when we do open up emotionally, our response is automatically classified into one of these areas.

"Women believe that all we think about is sex. Well...yes and no. Sex is on our minds a lot. We are constantly barraged with sexual temptation in the media, from newspaper adds to films. They hit us at our weak point. The guy who says he never notices is either lying or a walking cadaver.

"Our eyes are the problem. Men have innate visual scanners for anything that appeals sexually. Don't think we don't notice. The old adage that 'Women have to be in the mood and men have to be in the room' is true. Resistance is a struggle for Christian men.

"There is also a strong connection between a man's sex drive and his ego. Women need to know how they impact us. The way they dress, wiggle, look or touch us affects us. We struggle constantly with keeping our sex lives pure, especially when our wives are cold. Sometimes we don't want to be romantic—we just want to do it. Other times we need to know we are desired, loved and accepted. We enjoy having our wives take the initiative."

One man stated the problem well.

"I don't think women fully understand our sexual struggles because they just don't think the same. It's like trying to explain back pain to someone who has never had it. Something gets lost in the translation."

To continue from the questionnaires:

"We want women to know that although we are often too nonverbal and nonemotional, we care. We get the message that if we really loved our wives we'd adapt to their ways. Perhaps there is some truth in that."

In conclusion, here are eight statements from men that may leave you with some material for thought and discussion. Some of you may not be like these men, but here are their thoughts:

1. Men are not personal saviors. We cannot be the perfect fathers you had or hoped for when you were growing up. Too much is expected of us by women. We want you to receive more from the Lord so you will need less from us.

2. Men are the heads of the household and we need our wives' support with raising children. This concept is not a threat to the woman's authority—it supports it!

3. I feel that women are out to change us. We need to work together and allow our differences to complement each other.

4. I think women judge us for not processing the way they do. We tend to judge women for the same reason. Each wants the other to be more like themselves; therefore, we are both left with unfulfilled expectations.

5. My greatest struggle is understanding women. They are so complex. Just when I think I have a handle on the situation and I think I see a ray of hope in understanding my wife's feelings, she throws another log on the fire, which makes me feel hopeless. There are times when I feel like giving up and getting a divorce. But I don't believe in that! Then I feel maybe it's me, that I am super stupid. Yet when I see other men having the same problems, I realize I am not stupid. (Ignorant, maybe, but not stupid.) Anyway, I keep praying for God's wisdom.

6. Most men change when women respond to them with love and tenderness (gentleness—not loud defensiveness). Deep down men want intimacy—they just have not learned how to achieve it. We need to be loved.

7. I believe there is very little women don't really understand about men (and boys)! I feel rather transparent to my wife. I will now welcome her counsel.

An attorney who has practiced family law for more than 20 years summed up his conclusion after working with thousands of men, by saying:

8. After interviewing numerous men struggling with their marriages, there seems to be a fairly common pattern about what men think women *do not* understand about them. The most common answers are as follows: the need for time apart, relaxation, male bonding, sports involvement and physical needs.

The evening was dismissed and many men looked relieved to have been heard.

RESPONDING
TO THE "SPEECH"

Did you as a man identify with any of the previous comments? Which ones reflect your thoughts? What would you add to this list? What are you willing to change about yourself? If the woman in your life doesn't understand you, how will she learn if you don't tell her what you need? Isn't that where the conflict begins?

Some of the responses we heard from the conference indicate that many men struggle with "need" fulfillment. Dr. Willard Harley (partly out of his own experience) identified five basic needs men expect their wives to fulfill, and five needs women expect their husbands to fulfill.[1] Often the failure to meet each other's needs is based on ignorance rather than refusal. We may live in a country that has a high literacy level, but many of us are basically illiterate about marriage and the fine art of understanding our mates. There really is no reason for married couples not to be fulfilled today.

What basic areas of need and fulfillment did Harley report?

First, *men cannot do without sexual fulfillment.* Of course. This should not shock anyone.

The second need may surprise you. *Men want their wives to spend recreational time with them.* Recreational compatibility is very important, and it must be carefully cultivated because tastes vary. Men tend to enjoy activities that involve more risks and adventure than women do. Men often fear that if she joins him, his activities will be limited. Wives usually pressure husbands to spend their spare time with the family. This can build resentment. What works best for most couples is actually having his and her recreational activities, but putting an emphasis on "our" activities.

A third need according to Dr. Harley is for *the wife to be attractive.* This does not mean she has to be beautiful, but she should strive to maintain the level of attractiveness she had when they married. Of course, this should apply to men as well. I have seen as many men as women let themselves go after they marry.

A fourth need is for *peace and quiet*. Moms need time to recoup, recharge and rebound—so do dads. Couples need to discuss when this should occur so both are satisfied. Too often this becomes a source of tension and argument in marriage, and degenerates into a pursuit-withdraw conflict. I have often seen a man's needs fulfilled here while his wife strains for the relationship. Neglecting the concerns of either person will destroy a marriage.

The fifth area of need is *admiration*. One respondent shared his thoughts well:

> Many writers and therapists have pointed out the need that men have for admiration and respect. As one husband said, "Because of men's high need to accomplish, they are in need of more positive encouragement than most women seem to understand. I have observed some wives withholding praise from their husbands because they either thought their husbands did not need more praise or that others were doing a sufficient job already. Many wives fail to notice the desperate search by their husbands for honest acknowledgment of their efforts. One of the best gifts from God is a spouse who acknowledges, encourages and supports her partner as a natural habit. One of the blessings from my wife that has a great impact on me is when she speaks well of me to others. This is particularly true when she doesn't think that I am listening, or when I find out indirectly what she has said to someone. We all want to be well thought of, and when our wives become our "public relations managers" we experience honor from them, which is truly humbling.

Men thrive on honest admiration from women. We desperately need recognition and encouragement. Every man and every woman, however, needs to specifically identify his or her own unique needs and make a point of sharing them with their mates. Then they must make a point of meeting each other's expressed needs. One of the reasons people marry is to get their needs met.

ARE MEN FROM MARS?

Other writers have also discussed the needs of men. John Gray, in his best-seller *Men Are from Mars, Women Are from Venus,* identified some of the same male needs Dr. Harley expressed, then contrasted them with women's needs. Whereas women need caring, understanding, respect, devotion, validation and reassurance—men need trust, acceptance, appreciation, admiration, approval, and encouragement.[2] Dr. Gray provides some informative insights about the man-woman interaction and why some problems occur.

A wife often tries to improve her husband's responses or help him by offering unsolicited advice. His response? He feels unloved because he feels she is not trusting him. Suggestion: She could say, "I've got a suggestion if you're interested. You let me know if you are."

A wife may try to change or control her husband's behavior by talking about how upset she is or letting him know her negative feelings. Again, his response is, "She doesn't love me because she doesn't accept me the way I am." Suggestion: The requested change may be quite insightful, but it's not packaged in a way that is heard. Sharing the request in a positive way, pointing to the desired response and even expressing it in writing often works better. The husband could listen, reflect and ask his wife to say it differently.

A wife may not notice or acknowledge what her husband has done, but instead comments on what has not been accomplished. Naturally, he feels unappreciated and taken for granted. Suggestion: Men and women want their efforts to be recognized and valued. Appreciation is the best way to see the desired behavior continue.

A wife may correct what her husband says or does, and tell him what to do and how to do something. He does not respond well to directions, and he does not feel admired. Suggestion: Asking questions, or asking if he would like to hear an observation would be accepted better. When a wife shares her displeasure by asking questions that carry an accusatory tone implying "You blew it," she can count on a defensive response.

Common defense-producing questions are "How could you?" or "Why in the world did you do that?" The questions cause a husband to feel unaccepted, unapproved and unloved. Suggestion: Share your concern in a calm voice, saying, "I am upset and I don't want to be. Help me to understand what is happening. I need your perspective." This positive approach is more easily accepted than an accusation.

When a wife challenges, criticizes or corrects her husband's decisions or initiations (especially in front of others), he feels unloved, angry and humiliated. He wants to be encouraged to do things on his own. Suggestion: Again, ask if you can make an observation, or better still, ask some clarifying questions.

Dr. Gray also writes in detail about how men tend to respond inappropriately and what they can do differently. Both men and women need to refine their responses to better meet one another's needs.

Every concern and every issue mentioned by each man surveyed is legitimate in his own eyes. Men and women have carried misunderstandings about each other for years. Why? Simply because men rarely shared with their wives. The phrase we heard most often in our survey was, "You would think that she should just know." But why should a woman just know? She can't read your mind, and most men I know hate it when their wives make assuming comments indicating they are experts about their husbands.

A man's thoughts or feelings must be shared in words his wife can thoroughly understand. What is shared should be complete in details. A one-line summary is not sufficient. Some men have achieved success by providing either written detailed documents explaining what they would like to share or letters clarifying their needs, thoughts and feelings. Writing allows them to think it through carefully and makes it easier to share with their wives. Further discussion can then occur if desired.

TYPICAL, BUT DANGEROUS

When a man does speak out to be understood, it is important that he avoid two typical, destructive responses—anger and defensiveness. Unshared feelings gain intensity over time. When "stuffed" feelings are finally shared, either in a confrontation or by one's own initiative, they often surface in an overreaction.

Because men feel uncomfortable about being inadequately able to share their feelings, they overreact with anger or defensiveness.

Many men want to share, but at the same time they want to escape these very same feelings. So the rationalization begins. We tell ourselves, "Why talk about it? Is it going to do any good? Not really. Nothing will change." Or we maintain the attitude that this stuff will pass and we move on to something else.

It is easy to deny feelings or put them on hold. I see many men who use what I call a "thinking bypass" for their emotions. They replace feelings with thoughts and never get to the heart of their issues.

One of the most common reactions I have seen is substituting one feeling for another, such as anger for hurt or fear. Anger is less threatening than hurt or fear. But how can another person really know what is going on inside us if we don't share our real feelings? This is why feelings erupt. And because men have not been encouraged to be verbal or to increase their verbal skills, they often feel disadvantaged in sharing what is significant for women.

Women who engage in verbal gymnastics encourage men to resort to loudness, intensity and anger to compensate for their feelings of inadequacy. When men feel threatened, whether it's real or imagined, they try to override others.

The tendency to be defensive, to assume that you are being challenged or criticized, creates a roadblock to sharing what you want a woman to understand about you. Instead, do not interpret a question as a challenge; rather see it as an attempt to clarify and understand the issue. Also, don't judge her motive for asking the question.

THE REST OF THE STORY

Although this chapter is based on what men think women don't understand about men, men still don't understand much about women and marriage. This was especially evident from the numerous questions men asked their therapists or pastors in the counseling offices.

Many questions reflected deep frustrations about not knowing, not understanding or comprehending how to fix the problem. Many questions focused on how to change their wives.

We all need to be reminded that in a marriage relationship, one person's problem becomes a problem for both of them. Each inadvertently or consciously feeds the other's problem and may even reinforce it. Problems can be solved; they can be fixed.

Some of the statements and questions from the counseling survey reflect a longing for change. Men said they wanted their wives to change, and that's all right. We all want the person in our lives to change in some way. It's just that we usually solicit change in the wrong way. How?

We demand. Demanding is a losing proposition. It generates resistance. The pressure of our words and tone of our voice causes others to resist us.

We reinforce their negative responses. The very thing we don't want, we reinforce.

If the change you desire is not forthcoming, consider how you are requesting the change, why you want it, how intensely you want it and how committed you are to pursuing it.

Create an atmosphere for change by modeling it. Show positive changes in your own life that the other person can identify and appreciate. You will need to be persistent, sensitive, creative, loving and patient.

A SAMPLING OF CONCERNS

In our survey from the 700 counselors and pastors, numerous

questions and issues were raised about wives and marriage. The following is a sampling of the concerns and questions men asked in counseling. These responses indicate that both men and women struggle to understand the opposite gender.

- How can I (or you) get my wife to be less emotional?
- How can I get my wife to accept me the way I am?
- How can I get my wife to be as attentive and responsive to me as she is to her friends and family?
- How can I get my wife to respect me?
- How can I get my wife to stop nagging me?
- How can I meet the demands of a demanding, strong wife?
- How many times do I have to tell her "I love you"? After all, I married her, didn't I?
- I am not happy with my marriage. My wife pays all her attention to the kids and leaves no time or energy for me. What should I do?
- My wife is the only close relationship I have and she wants more autonomy. What do I do?
- My wife wants to talk, especially when I am tired. What can I do to get some peace and quiet?
- Now that my wife is working, how do I handle the fact that she has no time for me?
- Why can't my wife just be happy? She is always griping about something!
- Why can't my wife see that I love her? Look at all I do.
- Why does my wife always want to know all the small details of my day?
- Can you teach me how to meet my wife's needs?
- How can I love my wife as Christ loves the Church?
- How do I gain back my wife's confidence in me?
- How can I get her to understand my feelings? All she does is nag or cry.
- I am not sure I love my wife anymore. What do I do? No, there is no one else at this time.

It is interesting to note both the frustration expressed within this sampling of questions and the wording. Just reading the printed words could suggest blame and defensiveness. I have heard every one of these questions many times in my counseling office.

The answers or solutions I suggest are often neither new nor unique. Men confess that their wives have suggested the very same solutions, but they couldn't hear or listen to the suggestions at the time.

Many of the questions we just read reflect ignorance about some of the basics and fundamentals of wholesome relationships.

Many men could have avoided the need for counseling in their relationships had they taken the time to read a few books, or listen to some teaching about marriage and male-female relationships.

Women are more open to learning, growing and implementing changes in their lives. They read the books and attend the classes. The excuses some men give are weak and invalid: they don't have time, don't read much or know all they need to know. If a man is developing his life as God has called him to, he will eventually discover this information. God has made this information available to all men in His Word—we need only study it.

If you are struggling with the previously mentioned questions at this time, may I encourage you to make a commitment to grow and expand your understanding of women. God calls all husbands to love their wives as Christ loved the Church (see Eph. 5:25), and to live with their wives in understanding (see 1 Pet. 3:7). A good place to begin is the following reading list.

RECOMMENDED READING

Gray, John. *Mars & Venus Together Forever* New York: HarperCollins, 1994.

Harley, Willard. *His Needs, Her Needs*. Grand Rapids: Fleming H. Revell, 1986.

Smalley, Gary. *If Only He Knew*. Grand Rapids: Zondervan Publishing House, 1979.

Wright, H. Norman, and Oliver, Gary J. *How to Change Your Spouse, Without Ruining Your Marriage.* Ann Arbor: Servant Publications, 1994.

REFLECTING ON THIS CHAPTER

1. As a man, what three masculine traits would you most like for women to understand better?
2. Why do you think some men find it hard to put family interaction ahead of sports or hobbies? Is it natural for there to be some difference between men and women in this area?
3. Do you identify with the man who said, "At times I feel that a woman is out to try to change a man to her way of thinking"?
4. Do you agree or disagree with the common charge that men are afflicted with a "fragile male ego"?
5. If a wife habitually tries to "fix" the way her husband expresses himself, what is likely to occur?
6. Read Ephesians 5:25 and discuss how its teaching can be applied in a marriage.

Notes

1. Willard F. Harley Jr., *His Needs, Her Needs* (Grand Rapids: Fleming H. Revell, 1986), p. 12, adapted.
2. John Gray, *Men Are from Mars, Women Are from Venus* (New York: HarperCollins, 1992), pp. 140-141, adapted.

How a
Woman Can
Help a Man

Marriage has been called a relationship of shared hope, shared support and shared tasks.

Sometimes it works that way, but often marriage represents two separate unfulfilled people coexisting together. Wives long for more support from their husbands and husbands long for more support from their wives. Neither tells the other what they need, thus the marriage is lived out in silent disappointment and frustration.

Marriage can be fulfilling, but we must be willing to talk about our needs and share them in words that bring understanding and clarity to each other.

Numerous books have been written for women *by* women about what men really want or need. So we posed our survey question in a different way. We asked men, "What one thing would you like your wife to do that would indicate to you that she understands and accepts what you deal with in your daily life?"

The answers rolled in. The same answers were repeated again and again by the men who responded to our survey. On the pages that follow we will present 65 of the main responses from men of all ages and from all parts of the United States. Compare the responses of these men with your own. Ask yourself: Can any of their responses help me in my daily life?

If you are a woman reader, these responses may furnish insight about the man in your life. Ask him which of these statements fits his needs. If he says none of them apply, ask him to share what he *does* want from you.

The question again: *What one thing would you like your wife to do that would indicate to you that she understands and accepts what you deal with in your daily life?* The answers:

1. Show appreciation in recognizing the pressures men go through, and the responsibilities of provider and caretaker in the spiritual, emotional, financial, social, mental areas, etc. My focus is for the overall picture and goals. Oftentimes it is misunderstood and the appreciation is lost.
2. If she and I could sit down at the end of the day and review the highlights. To share what we really think, without having her making judgments about the people I work with. It would be nice to have a sounding board, someone to just bounce ideas off of, without judging and to get an honest opinion.
3. Just to say she understands with her words, hugs and actions.
4. A look directly in my eyes—and verbally or nonverbally stating, "I love you and am praying for you."
5. I think I am still a big kid at heart. I would like my wife to give me more encouragement regarding my business life and my home life. Maybe more "that-a-boys" or "thank you's" or "good job." I am at a level in my company where I don't get it at the office. I do get some appreciation at home, but that kid in me needs more.
6. Go to work with me and spend the whole day there to see what my life is really like.
7. To give me plenty of emotional and physical strokes that are positive. Touching, compliments, sexual play,

phone calls, notes, etc. To constantly reassure me that no matter what happens "out there in the world," she will always fully accept me in our relationship and our marriage.

8. To show genuine interest as she asks me how my day's work has gone.

9. Give me some space and time each evening to unwind from the day. Support my decisions.

10. Listen to me and verbally affirm her love and commitment to me in spite of my failures and fears.

11. Lovingly listen without passing judgment.

12. Their responding to us physically would help us to resist sexual temptation. (But ultimately it's up to us.) Knowing they want us would be helpful. Recognizing the stress level of life and doing some little things to relieve the pressure where possible. Even just listening or drawing us out to share the effects with them.

13. A little pampering and "babying" goes a long way. Also women need to be more patient listeners for us "quieter men."

14. I would love my wife to give me a hug, a kiss and ask me to share what's gong on in my head. And, after I'm done unloading all my concerns and worries to not offer advice, unless asked, but let's pray together for God's guidance. This would help me release all my anxieties to God and provide a clean heart for my family.

15. Continual affirmations that I am a good father/husband. Acknowledgment that I am doing the best I can, even if I don't quite measure up to desires or expectations. Don't compare me to other fathers! Give physical affection and let me know she is still glad she married me.

16. Affirmation, listening, encouragement to have time with quality Christian men (breakfast, sports, whatever).

17. That she would know we are very different and accept it. Not to put my interests down.

18. Just be happy with life and know that God and I love her.

19. Talk about it! This, of course, is a two-way street. I need to bring it up and let her know what my fears and struggles are.

20. Listen. Listening without being judgmental or biased. Listening and accepting. Listening just to understand me. Listening instead of criticizing.

21. I would like my wife to accept me for who I am. I don't want her to push me into being something I'm not. Have patience with me and help me to become a better me, not a different me.

22. Really understand that I do not have her perfectionistic personality and that while I try my best to do the things she wants done (to her standard), that I will never reach that level.

23. Before my wife can do one thing to demonstrate understanding and acceptance of my struggles, she needs to make time to talk in order to discover what they are. I know that this is a priority that we must share together. However, I do feel like a lower priority in my wife's life (after the needs of the children, her church commitments and time spent with her friends) than she is in mine. I guess if I had to pick one thing, I would like my wife to change her tone of voice when she speaks to me. Her predominant tone is critical, negative and belittling.

24. Just to have her assure me that she will support and love me no matter what happens. Even if I lose my job, or am uncertain about what to do next with my life. To affirm that God is in control and she is trusting Him to care for both of us.

25. Be more understanding of why small things are unimportant, like money, status, etc.

26. The one thing that I would like my wife to do is to encourage me. To create for me a place in her arms or in my home that is a shelter from the things I'm dealing with, not more demands or expectations. And not her personal suggestions of how I should deal with these things unless I solicit her opinion. Her encouragement would be in the form of words and actions.

Words like: "You're doing so well," "You can do it" and "I know what you do will be the best." And actions like finding ways to lighten my load; or just saying OK and doing something I suggest. Just agreeing would be a form of encouragement. Encouraging me to be myself would indicate to me that she accepts me, rather than always trying to change me. Wanting me different means not accepting who I am.

27. I guess for me it would be to work at taking the "log out of her own eye" so she could help me with mine. Then I could really trust her statements of understanding. I feel like I am working to get healthier and as head of the family it should probably start with me—I'm glad it has anyway. I feel she has yet to really start, so it's harder for her to comprehend and understand. When I'm more fully known by myself and then more fully known by her—then I feel her statements and support will mean more and I will be able to trust and receive them more. Too often now I feel that what I share comes back to "hit" me at a later date. I'm working to process that and deal with this issue with her as we speak.

28. At some point during the day we spend 10 minutes, not necessarily simultaneously, to write each other a love letter, communicating to each other the feelings we have had throughout the day, the feelings we experience upon writing the letter, and how appreciative we are of each other. Then for another 10 minutes, usually at the end of the day, we read each other's letters and discuss the feelings that arise. I would like her assurance that she will continue to listen attentively and our special times will continue together.

29. Sorry, I can't think of anything—my wife is actually very supportive. With three small children, heading up the children's ministries at our church, leadership in Bible Study Fellowship, her days are just as tough as mine. The thing I want to write is to not attack me as I walk in the door with questions or requests for

instantaneous decisions; but how would I feel if I had been with small children all day? Another possibility would be that she could give up some responsibilities to have more time for me. She often is still folding clothes through the 10 o'clock news, after which we retire. I seem to be last on her list oftentimes.

30. My wife talks to me at my level very well, but sometimes we are completely off. I like plans spelled out in detail and she hashes it out in her head. If she would slow down and outline her thoughts it would be easier for me to "read her mind."

31. Make mention of what I'm dealing with in prayer, especially our prayer time together.

32. If possible, visit work and help with a project or process (large or small). Or discuss current details at work and give suggestions on how I can be more effective (be a team member or cheerleader).

33. I'd like to continue to hear support that she gives to me. I wish I could praise her as much as she admires me. She is open with her affection for me. I can't ask for much more since she is so understanding. She knows me as much as herself.

34. Sally is my office manager—and a good one. Her gifts are for organization. I wish she could pick up on the "vision thing" a little more. I need to communicate it better.

35. Be more affectionate sexually and emotionally.

36. *One-a-Day Compliment*: a positive comment that acknowledges a good choice, a wise decision, a Christlike action, a leadership trait.

37. Listen to understand me with respect.

38. Accept my failures and encourage me anyway.

39. Respect me and be thankful for how I provide.

40. I don't know. I know my work habits (6:00 A.M.—4:00 P.M. at the office) are accepted as long as I stay in bounds. It seems very hard to stay in those bounds. My wife helps me to stay on target (hours). I find the first 10 minutes with my wife when I get home sets the stage for the rest of the evening. If she is upset with the

kids, I become hard on the children and cross.

41. I would like to have more positive contact: hugs, holding hands, touching.

42. *Give support and respect* (if the man earned it). The man, like all humans, wants recognition for his efforts. Do not (in public) undermine his authority.

43. I would like my wife not to get her identity and fulfillment from me. This puts too much pressure on me. When I can't fulfill her high expectations, she gets frustrated and passes that on to me! Christ is the only one for that position.

44. I am fortunate and have been blessed with a wife who does understand and accept all of my actions and reactions (excluding the struggle with sexual fidelity in marriage, which I have never discussed with her).

45. Become interested in work-related and other activities.

46. Say "I love you" often. To hold me and stroke my head.

47. Give me a break. In my job, I am a partner with my dad. It is just he and I. We do it all: sell, install, service! At the end of the day, sometimes I have had enough of people. When I get home, the last thing I need is for my wife to unload all of the problems of the kids and whatever else. We have four children, all boys! I know my wife needs to unload. I realize that and I am willing to listen, but there are times that I throw my hands up and walk away. I have told my wife my feelings on this, but it doesn't seem to do much good.

48. To be more willing to be my partner. To not think that she has to carry so much responsibility for how things go financially. She is very security oriented and illogically believes that an income from her job is all we can really rely on. She lost her job this year, and her grief about the loss has been consuming for both of us. She unsuccessfully tried to fill the loss with a graduate course—now she is searching for another job. I have yet to enjoy her being a wife in the classic sense of the word.

49. Ask me, draw me out gently, pray with me and for me.

50. Accept my choices and decisions without criticism, challenge or smart remark. I really have thought about these things and have tried to solicit input, tried to include the family. I feel like my position as husband and father is powerless, second-guessed, impotent; I either lash out or withdraw.

51. Positive statements which indicate I'm attempting to prioritize my work/home responsibilities in order to accomplish them.

52. Communicating more about the victories (closing the deal) and the defeats (abuse of people) of being a salesperson or of being a church leader (abuse).

53. Share her own spiritual growth and development as a person and listen to my concerns in this area. I feel very alone in my faith walk because she is not open to sharing this important area of our life together. However, it does not seem to be difficult for her to share it with other women (even strangers). Is she afraid to find out that I have similar struggles? She won't say, she just clams up!

54. Give space.

55. Initiate sexual intimacy now and then.

56. Initiate intimate conversation and physical contact.

57. I would love for my wife to ask questions that would lead to a greater understanding of who I am and what I have to deal with daily. I believe this would lead to a greater appreciation of me.

58. As a pastor, to know that she prays for me daily and is sensitive to the pressures that come with my profession. (By the way, she does this for me!)

59. Take time to look at the situations that are causing me worry or stress and then verbalize her concern. She loves me, prays for me, but seldom verbalizes this concern.

60. Carry out simple requests without asking "why?" or second-guessing what I've taken hours or days to think out.

61. Appreciate little things without chastising me for what I failed to do.

62. She is very sensitive toward the details of my life. It almost puts me to shame how much she thinks of and does for me.

63. Women like to vent their feelings to a listening spouse without editorials or comments. I would like my wife to draw out feelings about a situation but never editorialize or define what I mean. Such that if next Tuesday evening after thinking about a specific situation I may change my mind 180 degrees. I would like to be allowed to mull over things without being thought of as rude or disinterested.

64. To listen to and understand the fact that I do not want to die "with it all inside." There is too much to share to let it go. She needs to help in reaching the goal.

65. Defend me...not in a way that says I'm always right, but in a way that indicates she knows I'm really trying...there is a lot of criticism of men in today's society...I want to know my wife is on my side, not on the side that is critical, and I must say, I believe she is and does. For that I am grateful.

Overall, these statements tell us that wives need to change their approach to their husbands. Requesting change from each other is normal and important, especially when it is for the purpose of strengthening and enriching the marriage. The changes requested by most spouses are not for personality trait or feeling changes, but for changes in behavior. As a result, we cannot *not* change. As Christians, we must not be satisfied with ourselves as we are at the moment. Growth is a Christian responsibility (see 2 Pet. 1:5-7), and growth requires change.

MEN'S TOP 10 INTIMACY NEEDS

Earlier we shared some relational needs presented by Dr. Willard Harley Jr., author of *His Needs, Her Needs.* The author of *The Pursuit of Intimacy* also suggests the following are the top 10 intimacy needs in a marriage. When these needs are met, mutual satisfaction is realized by both husband and wife. These needs are not presented in order of importance, therefore, it may be helpful for you to list them in your own order of importance.

1. Attention

Attention means to think about the other person, to focus upon him or her by listening with your eyes and your ears in addition to showing interest, concern and support. It's a bit like entering into the other person's world.

What Paul said about the Body of Christ—the Church—applies also to marriage: "that there should be no division in the body, but that its parts should have equal concern for each other" (1 Cor. 12:25).

When you share a request for attention, say what you need, what the other person's attention will do for you and how it will improve the overall relationship. Above all, don't attack, indict or blame.

2. Acceptance

The best description I have heard of the quality of acceptance in love is more than 20 years old. Acceptance, this source said, is "an unconditional commitment to an imperfect person." True acceptance means deliberate, positive and ready reception. As Paul said, "Accept one another, then, just as Christ accepted you, in order to bring praise to God" (Rom. 15:7).

3. Appreciation and Praise

Every man and woman needs appreciation and praise. Appreciation *is gratefulness that is verbalized*. In most marriages, however, the norm is "to take for granted."

Make a list of every single helpful or positive thing your spouse does or has done. Then enumerate the times you have shared your appreciation for each one. Too often we are aware of what our partner *has not* done rather than what he or she has done. When we pay attention to their faults or defects, we just reinforce them. We must look for the positives and reinforce them with praise if we want them to continue.

Marriages that are satisfying are those in which there are five times as many positive exchanges as there are negative.[1] Remember what the apostle Paul said in 1 Corinthians 11:2: "I praise you for remembering me in everything and for holding to the teachings, just as I passed them on to you."

4. Support

The need for support in intimacy is described in the Bible as "bearing one another's burdens." This means discovering exactly how your partner would like to be supported—not doing what you think is best. It can also mean giving a hug rather than a solution, putting dinner on hold so your partner can unwind for a half hour or reflecting and clarifying your spouse's feelings rather than saying you are too tired to talk.

A counselee shared with me how his wife blessed him one day through her caring support and friendship. Phil, a man in his 30s, had been under intense pressure and stress for several weeks. His new job was a disaster because delays and unreasonable demands from his supervisor were wearing him down. Added to this, Phil and his wife had moved 2,000 miles away from home to take the job, and both sets of parents continued to express their displeasure about the move.

One particular day, everything was going wrong at work. In addition, Phil's parents called him at work to dump on him for abandoning them. As he was walking out at quitting time, his supervisor informed him that he would have to work the following Saturday.

When Phil arrived home he was totally dejected. His non-verbal signals screamed discouragement. He told me later, "I felt shattered, discouraged and unable to please anyone." He immediately headed for his chair and slumped into it in silence.

When Phil's wife entered the room, she could read his non-verbal signals and knew it had not been a good day. Phil explained what happened:

> Eileen just came over to me and stood behind me, gently stroking my hair and massaging my stooped shoulders. All she said was, "Would you like to talk

about it or not?" Her sensitivity, her touch, her willingness to give me the freedom to talk or not talk encouraged me so much. I didn't feel all alone anymore. I knew I had someone who would stand by me even in my discouragement. I felt blessed. In fact, I know I am blessed in having such a wife."

Many of the responses in our survey were from men requesting this kind of support. "Carry each other's burdens, and in this way you will fulfill the law of Christ" (Gal. 6:2).

5. Encouragement
The word basically means to give another person courage. Acts 18:27 defines the word "encourage": "to urge forward or persuade." In 1 Thessalonians 5:14, the word means to console, comfort and cheer up, especially the person who is discouraged and ready to give up.

In Hebrews 10:25, encouragement means to keep someone on his feet, who, if left to himself, would collapse. You are to be a cheerleader for your partner, encourage your partner by believing in him or her.

In Proverbs 31, we read about a highly functional and capable woman. Ministers often preach about this passage and use this woman as an example for other women. The reason she is such an ideal woman is often overlooked. You find it in verse 28: "Her husband boasts of and praises her" (*Amp.*). We are able to do our best when someone believes in us.

6. Affection
Affection is a basic ingredient of marriage. It can mean anything from a sexual interchange to a nonsexual touch. Touch is communication.

Affectionate touching generates the sensations of warmth, security and emotional satisfaction craved by every human being. Patting, stroking and caressing carry the nonverbal message of endearment and tenderness that we all need beginning at birth. That physical need does not diminish when we grow into adulthood.

No amount of cultural restriction or stereotyping can eliminate the need for physical contact; although Americans tend to be less "touchy" in relationships than people from other cultures. Travel to Europe, Africa or Asia and you might be surprised to find how adults hug, hold hands and lean against each other.

Helen Colton cites in her book *The Gift of Touch* (Putnam Publishing Group) the observations of a social scientist who contrasted the touching habits of Americans with those of the French. Within an hour's time, French friends touched each other about 100 times, while the Americans touched no more than 3 or 4 times.

Touching is an expression of affection. Women tend to desire affectionate touching more than men do. Men often perceive women's needs for physical contact as weakness, but touch is really a strength to all who welcome it. We men could learn much from what our wives already know about closeness.

The importance of warmth, tenderness and affection is powerfully portrayed by Donna Swanson in "Minnie Remembers."

> How long has it been since someone touched me? Twenty years I've been a widow. Respected. Smiled at. But never touched....Oh God, I'm so lonely. I remember Hank and the babies. How else can I remember them but together? Hank didn't seem to mind if my body thickened and faded a little. He loved it and he loved to touch it. And the children hugged me, a lot....Oh God, I'm lonely! God, why didn't we raise the kids to be silly and affectionate as well as dignified and proper? They drive up in their fine cars. They come to my room to pay their respects. They chatter brightly and reminisce. But they don't touch me. They call me Mom, or Mother or Grandma. Never Minnie. My mother called me Minnie. So did my friends. Hank called me Minnie, too. But they're gone. And so is Minnie.[2]

7. Approval
Every husband and wife looks for approval from a spouse.

Romans 14:18 reminds us, "because anyone who serves Christ in this way is pleasing to God and approved by men."

Approval is giving positive affirmation, or thinking and speaking well of someone. It can be expressed in a word or a look.

God models approval for us in His Word. What he said to Moses, He says to us: "I am pleased with you" (Exod. 33:17). God takes pleasure in you! He even rejoices over you in song (see Zeph. 3:17).

Married couples are to approve of each other. You have a choice: You can look for something to approve of or you can look for something for which to disapprove. "Love," Paul wrote, "is ever ready to believe the best of every person" (1 Cor. 13:7, *Amp.*).

8. Security

Security involves trust. It means you can depend on the one you trust. You can rely upon that person's word. You can count on that person to back you and to praise you not only in your presence, but also when you are not there. You know that person is doing what is best for you. Psalm 15:4 speaks of people who inspire security and dependability by saying, "They keep their promises, no matter what the cost" (*CEV*).

9. Comfort or Empathy

Having someone who understands us, identifies with us and can therefore comfort us is an important need. It is also an admonition from Scripture: "Therefore encourage each other with these words" (1 Thess. 4:18); "Rejoice with those who rejoice; mourn with those who mourn" (Rom. 12:15).

Comfort consoles in a way that touches the heart of the other person. Comfort can be different for each of us, therefore we need to understand what brings comfort to our own mate. Comfort can be expressed in words, silence, actions, sex, holding each other, etc.

When you empathize with someone, you enter into the experience with that person. You gently coming alongside the other person, matching his or her pace. You see through the other person's eyes. When you fail to empathize, your partner feels disappointed and rejected.

When a man is hurting, his wife needs to be especially sensitive to his needs. It is important for a wife to determine whether her husband needs privacy or attention. It is equally important for her husband to tell his wife what he needs. Offering him unsolicited advice often makes matters worse. It sends the message that he can't or won't figure out the problem for himself. Because being competent is important to him, he tends to be touchy about this. He hears it as a criticism. Instead, his wife should ask him if he would like to hear her suggestions.

Men should also restrain themselves from offering solutions when women are hurting and emotionally down. Most women just want and need to talk, to be heard and to be emotionally validated. They don't need to have their comments corrected either.

The following statements do not convey empathy:

141

"Why are you upset about that?"
"Don't worry so much about that."
"Oh, you shouldn't feel that way. Look at it logically."
"Here's what you need to say."
"Why in the world do you let them do that to you?"
"I'll handle it."

A man who has learned not to offer solutions, immediate feelings or downplay his wife's problems has arrived. He is now wise!

Keep in mind if you are trying to be comforting or empathetic that men and women tend to handle their problems and struggles differently. Exceptions do exist, but in general the following differences will be prevalent.

Men usually need to put the problem on the back burner, think about it and find a solution. Men do not readily have answers to their wives' questions or even their own problems when asked. When men are upset or stressed, talking may not be helpful. Men tend *not* to want to say anything they might regret later. Silence (for a while) may be necessary.

Men who respond to the question "What's wrong?" with "I'm all right," "It's fine," "Nothing," "It's no problem" or "It's no big deal" are sending the message that they want space or silent acceptance.

Women usually want to talk about their issues because talking helps them resolve their problems. Women are seldom looking for agreement; rather, they want to be heard. Questions help them figure out their problems. Women tend to share their negative feelings out loud as a means of discovering positive feelings.

A man's best approach for demonstrating empathy for his wife is to encourage her to talk. Take the initiative. Give her permission to be upset and to talk longer than you might think necessary. You don't need to be upset because she is upset. That won't help her. If you are tempted to set her straight or clarify the facts, forget it. If you don't know what to say, tell her so. Never, but never, challenge or correct her feelings. You can make a choice to stay calm, so stay calm. Remember that 1 negative comment can wipe out 20 positive comments.

The best responses a wife can make when her husband has responded with empathy are; "Thank you for listening," "Boy, it sure helps me feel better now that that's out," "Thanks for taking the time to help me figure things out," "It helps my mood to talk and have you listen to all that stuff. I see it differently now."[3]

10. Respect

Although both men and women need respect, men seem to need it more than women. When you respect people, you value them. You have a high regard for them and you honor them.

"Love each other with brotherly affection and take
delight in honoring each other" (Rom. 12:10, *TLB*).

Belittling, correcting and giving too much unsolicited assistance diminishes respect. Paul wrote:

However, let each man of you [without exception]

love his wife as [being in a sense] his very own self;
and let the wife see that she respects and reverences
her husband [that she notices him, regards him,
honors, prefers him, venerates and esteems him;
and that she defers to him, praises him, and loves
and admires him exceedingly] (Eph. 5:33, *Amp.*).

If this advice were followed by all husbands and wives, I
could retire from marriage counseling.[4]

CHOICES THAT ARE
YOURS TO MAKE

The needs of husbands and wives described in this chapter
correspond to many of the issues I have encountered in counseling with couples throughout the past 30 years. Often meeting each other's needs is a matter of choice.

The problems of misunderstanding, lack of understanding,
disharmony and failure to adjust to each other's uniqueness
exist for three reasons: the lack of *information*, the lack of
application and the lack of *motivation* to follow through on the
first two.

If you came to me for marriage counseling, I would give
you a choice. I would suggest you both come in for counseling and spend at least 10 to 20 sessions working on your relationship. (I would probably meet with you each week and the
cost would be from $800 to $1,500. That is not too much to
invest in a marriage when you consider the thousands of dol-
lars a divorce costs, as well as the economic and emotional
devastation that lasts for years afterward.)

Or I would suggest that both husband and wife read the
three books listed in a later paragraph, apply what you read,
discover new ways of relating and save most of the cost I just
mentioned. (You would have to pay for the books and your
weekly dates.)

What dates? I didn't mention those, did I?

It is important for a healthy marriage to continue to
grow—forever. *Love does not have to die.* It wants to live. We
kill it through neglect. We inadvertently become marital hit

men or women. Dates help to keep love alive.

The three books I recommend are: *How to Change Your Spouse, Without Ruining Your Marriage* by H. Norman Wright (Ann Arbor: Servant Publications, 1994); *Secrets of a Lasting Marriage* by H. Norman Wright (Ventura, Calif.: Regal Books, 1995); and *Mars & Venus Together Forever* by John Gray (New York: HarperCollins, 1994).

I have heard more men than women say they don't read books. That's too bad. The main reasons I have seen for not reading are basically pride and laziness. For a Christian man, those reasons don't fly! They are counter to all that God asks men to be. Look at the book of Proverbs! It will set you back on your heels.

As a man, I don't know everything. At times I thought I did, but I don't. I have discovered how great it is to learn from others, including my wife.

Too much good information is available today for us to live in marital ignorance. The choice is there. We can stay the way we are, stagnate and even lose our marriages. Or we can assume the role of a student, and become all that we, our partners and God want us to be.

It's possible for you!

REFLECTING ON THIS CHAPTER

1. Why do you think it is sometimes hard for husbands and wives to tell each other explicitly what they need?
2. As time allows, select and discuss several of the 65 responses from this chapter that fit your own situation.

Notes
1. John Gottman, *Why Marriages Succeed or Fail* (New York: Simon and Schuster, 1994), pp. 41-47, 57, adapted.

2. Donna Swanson, *Minnie Remembers* (Nashville: Upper Rooms, 1978).
3. John Gray, *Men Are from Mars, Women Are from Venus* (New York: HarperCollins, 1992), pp. 20-25, 70-80, adapted. See also John Gray, *What Your Mother Couldn't Tell You and Your Father Didn't Know* (New York: HarperCollins, 1994), pp. 140-148 and 200-210, adapted.
4. Dr. David and Teresa Ferguson and Dr. Chris and Holly Thurman, *The Pursuit of Intimacy* (Nashville: Thomas Nelson Publishing, 1993), pp. 46-56, adapted.

MEN AND
SPIRITUAL
FULFILLMENT

Men have spoken throughout this book and exposed their private lives. But has the silence been fully broken? Have they shared everything? Could anything significant not have been addressed?

Yes, one of the most personal issues for a man: *his spiritual life—his relationship with God.* This subject was scarcely mentioned or alluded to in either of the surveys. Admittedly, men were not asked to address it directly, but other topics not explicitly mentioned did surface. This one, however, did not. Its absence from their comments is eloquent testimony to the reserve most men feel about sharing their spiritual lives.

The spiritual development of a man's life reflects his solution to the struggles left to him by Adam. It reverses the residue from the Fall. It transitions man from being a wounded male to a whole male. It is also the key to enabling man to be all he was meant to be in his relationship with a woman—to be an ally rather than an adversary.

As a man grows in the wisdom and knowledge of God, his defensive skin can be shed as he understands who and what he is and can be. Jesus Christ offers him freedom that can release him from reserve and passivity. Godliness does not mean no more struggles—it means the power to face them is now available. It also means fully experiencing the benefits of being created in the image of God.

Men do want more for their lives; and God wants more for them. Men want to be significant; and God gives them significance. Men want to live purposeful lives; and God gives them purpose. God fills men's lives with destiny and stretches men to fulfill their destinies through serving Him. There is more to life than focusing on self. Men were created for a purpose, and only in Christ can they find it.

WHEN MEN ENCOUNTER JESUS

When a man encounters Jesus Christ, he encounters a real man, a masculine man, one who faced all of life's difficulties and temptations and conquered them all. Why wouldn't every man have a desire to have the strength and character of Jesus Christ? Look at what He did in fulfilling the Ten Commandments:

> Jesus was the only one to fulfill the law which means we can live within the boundaries of the law.
>
> Jesus never put any god or indeed anything before His Father.
>
> Jesus never constructed materially or mentally an idol in the form of anything; He worshiped God, as He taught others, "in spirit and in truth."
>
> Jesus never misused the Father's name but instead "hallowed" it.
>
> Jesus kept the Sabbath day holy.
>
> Jesus unfailingly honored His earthly father and mother.
>
> Jesus never indulged in murderous, hateful thought.
>
> Jesus never engaged in mental adultery, much less physical adultery.

Jesus never stole, or even had a larcenous thought.

Jesus never once bore false testimony—no slander or gossip or flattery or untrue words—only perpetual truth.

Jesus never coveted anything except another's spiritual well being.[1]

When a man encounters Jesus Christ, he is also encountering God. Jesus was and is God. In a way that defies explanation and understanding with our finite minds, Jesus is both God and man.

A Manly Cause

When a man encounters Jesus, he is also encountering a new cause and purpose for his life as well as a new potential for fulfillment of his own manhood. We were created for a purpose, to express something more than ourselves. Dr. Joe Stowell, president of Moody Bible Institute, spells it out for us:

Many of us fear that...if we fully yield the reins of our life to Christ, He will take away our manhood. Victims of a demasculinized portrait of Christ, we have forgotten that His perfect blend of divinity and humanity was expressed through existence as a man. He was the perfect expression of manhood. While that meant He had a special compassionate side, He also displayed strength and power. Enough strength and power to attract strong men as His followers. Enough so that they even gave up their careers and personal ambitions and followed Him.

Jesus Christ does not at all diminish our manhood. He emerges through the distinct qualities of our maleness to create a fuller and richer expression of what a man can be.

He redefines our manhood by replacing the motivations of our world with new guidelines for success. He directs our manhood along the path of ultimate significance. He takes our instincts to protect, provide, conquer, and accumulate, and points them in productive directions.[2]

Have you ever looked into the eyes of a man who has a cause? A graphic, penetrating picture of four horsemen hangs on a wall at Focus on the Family headquarters in Colorado Springs. Many people own a print of this picture. You can't just give it a casual glance. It won't let you do that. It reaches out and draws you in. The four riders are riding toward you. They are not just loping along without a purpose. In his book *Tender Warrior*, Stu Weber provides the best description of this picture of the four horsemen:

> What was it about that picture? I can tell you what I saw. These cleared-eyed riders had tamed the beasts beneath them...and within them. They were riding together as comrades. Not alone. Not isolated. They had understood that masculinity was made for connection. They rode together upstream. Fully equipped to face the elements. You could see their breath on the cold fall morning. They rode together as friends and soul-mates and warriors, against the force of the current, into the cold wind and exhilarating in it.
>
> But there's more to it. There's a story behind it. Those men were going somewhere. There was something out there, ahead of them, beyond them. They were men on a mission. They were going for it with everything in them.
>
> That's what struck us—an image of men with a calling. Carried along by something beyond themselves. Willing to face the obstacles. Willing to buck the current and the wind and the dangers. Willing to die, if necessary.
>
> Focus on the Family commissioned that painting to commemorate four men who were key to that organization. They were killed in a plane crash on their way home from a ministry retreat. Four laymen protecting—through their ministry

involvement—the spiritual values of a whole nation. Four men who were teaching through life and words the principles of the living God—lived out in their homes and their neighborhoods. Four men who were loving and caring for their own and beyond their own. Men who were other-oriented, not self-oriented. Men on a mission paying the price. That's the overarching characteristic of Christ's life. He was a man on a mission. A mission that mattered forever. And until you and I orient ourselves to the calling of Christ, we will never truly be men.[3]

Some men merely drift through life; others live with a purposeful mission. Some men grow spiritually; others remain stunted.

The Struggle to Grow

Growing spiritually doesn't just happen; it is a struggle. I asked a number of men to share what their spiritual lives and experiences had been. What a wide range of responses they offered, from despair to a sense of desire for growth and joy. Perhaps you can identify with some of their comments:

> For years I have tried to do the Christian thing and pray and read the scriptures. I start out with good intentions, but when I pray my mind drifts and I end up daydreaming. When I read the Scriptures, I've read it. But that's all. I don't get anything out of it. Why do it?
>
> I pray, now and then. I'm not regular, but I don't see why I need to be. When I need Him, I'll talk to Him and I'll know He's there. I'm really busy and stressed in my life with my job. So I don't need a lot of extra activity and church involvement in my life right now.
>
> Each year we go to a retreat with other couples. I come away each year all fired up and ready to go. I pray, pray with my wife, read the Scripture and

it lasts awhile, but over time it all just gradually
fades away. I get a lot out of it when I'm doing it.
It's great. I can always see a change in my life. I
clean up my act. So why can't I stick with it?

Many men ask: "Why can't I make it spiritually?" Some of
their hindrances are legitimate, such as lack of a role model,
lack of a spiritual mentor, inconsistent Christians, fear of being
vulnerable and the struggle of moving from independence to
dependence upon God. This latter struggle is ironic because
only in becoming dependent can a man really be set free!

Men avoid the spiritual dimension of their lives more than
women do. One denomination, for example, claims the sub-
scribers to their two devotional magazines are predominant-
ly women. It is estimated that 85 percent of Christian books
are purchased and read by women. Church services have
more women in attendance than men. More women than men
believe that faith and religion can answer the problems of our
time.[4]

It Can Be Done!
Let's look at what can be done, instead of focusing on why
spiritual development is such a struggle for men. Some men
are successful in their spiritual lives. The following is a snap-
shot of the devotional and spiritual lives of several men who
shared their insights with us:

- Prayer—conversation with God, through much of
  the day. Listen to many radio biblical teachers.
  Personal scripture study and personal praise and
  worship.
- I read the Bible every day and pray frequently during the day. Most of my readings are books of
  faith. (*Guideposts* or other Christian literature.)
  Each morning my wife and I have corporate devotions for about 45 minutes. We start our day with
  these devotions.
- Bible reading three days a week. Devotional verse
  each morning.

- Daily, I attend daily mass; pray as a family; read devotional book of Scripture readings. I regularly pray about events and encounters in life and ask for God's will and His intercession.
- About 30 to 45 minutes of Bible reading and reading devotional books every morning, followed by praying with my wife and then prayer alone for 10 minutes or so. Prayer throughout the day as things come up.
- Five days out of seven I study the Word looking for the main idea of 10 to 30 verses. I make questions and observations on each verse, then write an application for my own life. Then I pray, on my knees.
- Twenty to 30 minutes about four to five days a week. Chapter reading or subject related. Used *Family Walk* and *Keys for Kids* for family devotions for 11 years straight.
- My personal devotional life: Right after I became a Christian in high school I was discipled by a gentleman who really got me interested in studying the Word on a daily basis. I would sneak out of my bedroom in the early morning. My mom was an early riser, as am I, and I would sneak out just so she wouldn't know I was awake yet. (I don't know why I did this.) But I'd sneak into another room that we had where we had a partition in the room and had prayer requests and Bible verses that I was trying to memorize posted on the back of this partition and I would have my own private time with God. It was like a prayer closet, I guess you would say. I am not a big Scripture memorizer; I am a journaler. I talk about my experiences and what I'm learning from the work of God and other people around me. I take incessant notes of sermons, at conferences and other things. So my personal devotional life consists of reading the Word, sometimes working through workbooks. I like to use workbooks and things like that more than I do

reading on my own; and then journaling and looking over past notes from other things. Right now,
it's pretty erratic. I am not in the Word daily as I'd
like to be. I am in the Word weekly, which is the
best way to put it. It's part of my weekly life.

- I try to spend some time each day reading
  Scripture and praying. I usually miss Saturdays,
  because by the time I get up the kids are up and
  the day is off and running. In order for me to have
  time with the Lord it seems that it must be early in
  the morning. Many times I will read and pray
  while in the bathroom, or while I am eating a bowl
  of cereal in the morning.

- I pray constantly, acknowledging God's presence.
  I study the Bible once a week and read the Bible
  two to four times a week in a quiet time type of
  atmosphere. I try to spend time in worship at least
  twice a week.

- Over the past several years I have developed a discipline in my devotional life which I had never
  previously experienced. I found that the single
  most important factor in improving my walk with
  the Lord is to establish a regular, disciplined time
  of meeting with Him through Scripture and
  prayer. I had experimented with setting aside daylight or late night time, but I have been most successful with early morning worship time.

- I would describe my devotional life as very strong.
  While I still have brief periods of neglect lasting
  for days and sometimes weeks, I generally spend
  30 to 60 minutes each morning in Bible reading,
  worship and prayer. I find that I am more conscious of the Lord's presence in my life throughout
  the day, and I speak with Him frequently during
  my work activities. I read one chapter of Proverbs
  daily, along with some Psalms and other selected
  scriptures. I also read one or two books per week
  related to spiritual matters.

- During my quiet times in the morning, I frequently use my guitar as part of worship (although with four children, such private times are increasingly difficult to find!). I have found that praying out loud is much more effective than silent prayer, and I usually pray while kneeling or standing with hands outstretched.

SPIRITUAL ATHLETES

What does it take for a man to grow and develop spiritually? Consider this: *it takes sweat and stripping.* If that doesn't capture your attention, I don't know what will!

First Timothy 4:7 provides a key phrase for anyone who wants to grow spiritually: "Train yourself to be godly." The word "train" means to train naked. It is the word from which we get the English word *gymnasium.* In traditional Greek athletic competition, the athlete wore no clothes so he wouldn't be hindered in any way. So originally the word meant to exercise naked. The Greek athlete stripped off everything that might keep him from winning.

Exercise or training results in sweating. So Paul is calling every man to produce spiritual sweat! This is what it takes to grow. We must eliminate habits, behaviors, involvements and even associations that can keep us from moving ahead spiritually. Some of them may be so ingrained that we will have to "sweat" to strip them away, but anything that weighs us down has to go. As the book of Hebrews says:

> Since we have such a huge crowd of men of faith watching us from the grandstands, let us strip off anything that slows us down or holds us back, and especially those sins that wrap themselves so tightly around our feet and trip us up; and let us run with patience the particular race that God has set before us (Heb. 12:1, *TLB*).

That is pretty clear isn't it? Growth takes discipline and sweat. I learned this back in 1979. I went through a burnout, clear and simple. I overdid it, and I did it to myself. I didn't allow enough time to recuperate between seminars, teaching, counseling and writing. The problem was that I enjoyed everything I was doing. I tended to be overaccommodating so I didn't say *no* enough. I was running on empty with nothing more to give, and my airplane crashed.

I took time off, played more and finally started a regular exercise program. Younger friends encouraged me to take up racquetball (probably so they could whip me). So at 42 I started playing racquetball. I really enjoyed it, but I ached and sweated! I also bought an exercycle and began riding 10 miles a day. I ached even more, and the sweat poured off. So did a few pounds. Sixteen years later I'm still at it, although with a little less intensity as I approach 60.

It is amazing what 16 years of practice on a racquetball court can do for timing, skill, coordination and placement. The same number of years spent on an exercycle did a lot for my legs and endurance, as well as dropping my heart rate of 80 down to 58. That is what discipline will do.

Becoming a godly man takes discipline, too. Kent Hughes shares an interesting perspective about this:

> The word discipline may raise the feeling of stultifying constraint in some minds—suggesting a claustrophobic, restricted life. Nothing could be further from the truth! The obsessive, almost manic discipline of Mike Singletary liberates him to play like a wild man on the football field. Hemingway's angst over the right word freed him to leave a mark on the English language second only to Shakespeare. The billion sketches of the Renaissance of the great Michelangelo set him free to create the skies of the Sistine Chapel. Churchill's painstaking preparation freed him to give great "impromptu" speeches and brilliant ripostes. The disciplined drudgery of the musical greats released their genius. And, brothers in Christ, spiritual discipline frees us from the gravity of this present age and allows us to soar with the saints and angels.[5]

STAGES OF GROWTH

When men begin to grow in faith, they often go through four stages of relating to God. The first stage is the *Give me* stage. We all start there. We want to receive. That is our focus, and it is natural; but we must guard against being demanding.

As we grow, we move from *Give me* to *Use me*. The emphasis on getting is replaced with the desire to be used by God. Sometimes the desire to *do* outruns the depth of knowledge and ability. This heart attitude is positive, but it must be properly guided by a more mature believer. The action of doing something for God could become too intense and leave a man empty.

The third stage is a desire to move from *Give me* and *Use me* to *Make me more like Jesus*. We desire not only to receive from our Lord, and to be useful to Him, but we also want His ways to become our ways.

The fourth stage reflects a love for God and a desire for spiritual intimacy. We want to *Know God and know Christ.*[6]

As you reflect on these four stages, keep in mind that a mature Christian will function at all four levels. We will continue to receive from the Lord, but we will also spend ourselves in His service, becoming more like Him and coming to know Him and His Son intimately.

At what stage are you functioning? To what degree is each stage a part of your life?

LIFE-CHANGING ASPECTS OF GROWTH

A man's spiritual growth is cultivated through attentive planning and focus. The following disciplines should be maintained when a man becomes serious about growing in the Lord.

The Counter-Culture Man
Living a Christian life will necessitate some counter-culture behavior and thought patterns. A man living for Jesus Christ may be viewed by this world as an outlaw. Scripture warns:

> Don't copy the behavior and customs of this world,
> but be a new and different person with a fresh
> newness in all you do and think (Rom. 12:2, *TLB*).

"Don't copy the behavior...of this world." A godly man is
called to be holy.

> You shall be holy to me, for I the Lord am holy,
> and I have set you apart from all other peoples, to
> be mine. (Lev. 20:26, *TLB*).

To live a life committed to Jesus Christ means thinking with
a Christian mind-set. It involves limiting what is fed into your
mind so nothing at odds with a Christian mind-set can enter.

A passage to guide a man in his pursuit of healthy
Christian thinking is this:

> And now, brothers, as I close this letter let me say
> this one more thing: Fix your thoughts on what is
> true and good and right....Think about all you can
> praise God for and be glad about (Phil. 4:8, *TLB*).

The Saturated Man

You must saturate yourself with God's Word if you want to
become a complete man. Saturation bombing in war is often
used to totally obliterate enemy positions in certain areas.
Planes continuously drop load after load of bombs in a back-
and-forth, crisscross pattern until every inch of land has been
covered. Similarly, you need to allow the Holy Spirit to saturate every inch of your heart and mind with the blessed truth
of who you are and what you are becoming in Christ.

Years ago I was fishing on a lake with one of my dogs, a
sheltie. He was perched on the bow of the boat, enjoying the
ride with his nose in the wind. I was headed into a cove at full
speed. Suddenly I changed my mind about fishing there,
swung the boat around and reversed my direction. The
abrupt course change caused my dog to lose his balance, and
he went flying into the lake. I don't know who was more surprised—my sheltie or me!

I swung the boat around to where he was swimming (he wasn't too happy with me at that moment) and cut the engine. I picked him out of the water, but I didn't lift him into the boat right away because he was totally soaked. He didn't have a dry spot of fur or skin. I held him away from the boat, gently squeezed his coat to eliminate most of the water and only then brought him into the boat safe and sound.

My new dog is quite different from my sheltie. He weighs three times as much as my sheltie did. And because he is a golden retriever, he loves playing in water. He doesn't get soaked. His coat actually repels the water. When he emerges from the water he appears wet, but the water doesn't penetrate his thick coat. Within a short time, it looks as though he never went swimming.

Some of us are negatively thick coated like my retriever. God's truth has never thoroughly penetrated our outer layer and deeply influenced us. We haven't been fully soaked. For growth to occur, we must saturate ourselves in God's truth.

Reading, studying and memorizing God's Word will change any man.

When I was a teenager, I was involved in memorizing Scripture, and it has helped more times than I can remember. On several occasions when I was facing a temptation and struggling with a decision, Scripture I had memorized came into my mind right at that moment. Usually it was 1 Corinthians 10:13:

> But remember this—the wrong desires that come into your life aren't anything new and different. Many others have faced exactly the same problems before you. And no temptation is irresistible. You can trust God to keep the temptation from becoming so strong that you can't stand up against it, for he has promised this and will do what he says. He will show you how to escape temptation's power so that you can bear up patiently against it (*TLB*).

That passage was a lifesaver for me as a young man. Throughout the decades of adulthood (I'm 58 at this writing), I did not make a consistent attempt to memorize God's Word. Recently, however, a friend at a family camp shared a section from his new book *Seeking Solid Ground*, which is about Psalm 15. He gently challenged us to memorize this psalm. It explains how to get the most out of life and the kind of person who does.

I don't know why, but I accepted the challenge. It took more work at my age. I committed just two or three minutes each morning and the passage became mine. Now when I wake up at night I often quote it silently. I quote it when I'm driving. The words are reassuring. They keep me alert, on track for God. I'm working on another passage now. I don't want to stop.

Gifted men, strong men, busy men, risk-taking men let God's Word shape their lives.

A Mentor for Men

Men need mentors, guides, examples. Let me give you one. Some of you reading this book won't remember World War II, but I do. Our world was totally dominated and influenced by that war. You may recall the names of some of the famous generals of that day such as MacArthur, Patton, Eisenhower.

Not too many people, however, remember Lieutenant General William K. Harrison. He was the most decorated soldier in the 36th Infantry Division—the first American to enter Belgium at the head of the allied forces. When the Korean War broke out, he served as chief of staff in the United Nations. President Eisenhower chose him to head the difficult negotiations to end the conflict.

This man was rugged, insightful and busy. Yet not too busy to read God's Word. William K. Harrison began a lifelong practice when he was a 20-year-old cadet at West Point of reading through the Old Testament once a year and the New Testament four times a year. During the years of global conflict, he continued this practice until his eyes failed him at the age of 90. By then he had read the Old Testament 70 times and the New Testament 280 times! He was known as a godly man, and he led the officers' Christian Fellowship for 18 years.[7]

Busy? This man was busy, but he fed on God's Word every day. His knowledge of the Bible successfully navigated him through all of his daily problems.

What about yourself, as a man? Does business override knowing God's Word? Do TV sitcoms or sports take priority over God's Word? Does His Word guide each of your daily decisions? Our goal is reflected in Psalm 119:97-100.

> Oh, how I love them [God's commandments]. I think about them all day long. They make me wiser than my enemies, because they are my constant guide. Yes, wiser than my teachers, for I am ever thinking of your rules. They make me even wiser than the aged (*TLB*).

If you will spend just 10 minutes a day reading and studying God's Word and 10 minutes reading devotional material, you will grow spiritually. Much more devotional material is available today than years ago. Discover your own preference. Max Lucado and Ken Gire have influenced me most in their writings about our Lord. I have also been inspired and challenged by the daily devotions written by Lloyd Ogilvie. Books, magazines, monthly devotionals, Promise Keeper materials all abound today. The problem is not accessibility or availability of material—it is the commitment to use it.

The Potential of Prayer
In addition to the study of God's Word, prayer is another life-changing discipline. Prayer is listening to God speak. Are you surprised by that statement? Most people say prayer is talking *to* God, not *with* God. They may add a token "Oh yeah, it's also listening to Him."

Kent Hughes describes the effect of prayer on Christian character when he says:

> Prayer is like a time exposure to God. Our souls function like photographic plates, and Christ's shining image is the light. The more we expose our lives to the white-hot sun of His righteous life (for, say, five, ten, fifteen, thirty minutes or an hour a day), the more His image will be burned into our

character—His love, His compassion, His truth, His integrity, His humility.[8]

Perhaps some men have difficulty with prayer because they are take-charge, type *A*, aggressively masculine personalities. In contrast, prayer requires that we let God take charge. Prayer is not a time when we dictate to God. It is a time when we allow ourselves to be changed into what He wants us to be. Prayer is fellowship with God. We don't pray to change God's mind; we pray to understand what His mind and will is for us.

If you are like me, sometimes you want to pray and even need to pray, but not much happens. It could be a mental block or maybe you're just not sure for what to pray. That is the time to ask the Holy Spirit to guide you and to show you how to pray and for what to pray. Are most men too "macho" to ask for and submit to such guidance?

> And in the same way—by our faith—the Holy Spirit helps us with our daily problems and in our praying. For we don't even know what we should pray for, nor how to pray as we should; but the Holy Spirit prays for us with such feeling that it cannot be expressed in words. And the Father who knows all hearts knows, of course, what the Spirit is saying as he pleads for us in harmony with God's own will (Rom. 8:26,27, *TLB*).

We are urged to pray for everything.

> Don't worry about anything; instead, pray about everything; tell God your needs and don't forget to thank him for his answers (Phil. 4:6, *TLB*).

> Here are my directions: Pray much for others; plead for God's mercy upon them; give thanks for all he is going to do for them (1 Tim. 2:1, *TLB*).

Incidentally, your prayers do not have to be long, elaborate and flowery. Nor should you compare your prayers with anyone else's. Using your pastor's prayers as a comparison will only hinder you.

Prayer needs to be continual and persistent. It is not just for a certain time of day nor is it limited to a particular place. Pray continually, as 1 Thessalonians 5:17 states: "Always keep on praying" *(TLB).*

Some men have a set time and a set place for prayer. That's it. Nowhere else. Setting a time and place is good, but it is also restrictive. Praying continually can mean going through each day with the attitude, "I can pray at anytime and in any place for any situation." Pray one-sentence prayers as you drive along or just before an important meeting.

A Christian TV host influenced me with his "eyes open" spontaneous prayer. When he was struggling with a portion of a show, right in the midst of the program and with his eyes open, he would pray. Everyone was accustomed to this practice. It was natural, genuine and brief.

Be persistent in praying for yourself and for others. Always, always be praying. Prayer is work. It takes effort. It will change lives—most of all, your own.

The Power of Fellowship

Godly men are not to exist in isolation. You need others to study with you and pray with you—people to whom you are mutually accountable. If you are married, your spiritual journey is to be taken with your companion—your spouse.

If couples would join together spiritually, there would be no coming apart. Imagine what a world we would have then—a restoration—the Garden revisited—Adam and Eve, trusting allies.

REFLECTING ON THIS CHAPTER

1. Do you think Dr. Joe Stowell's statement is true of most men?—"Many of us fear that...if we fully yield the reins of our life to Christ, He will take away our manhood."

2. Are you satisfied with the number and quality of

163

goals or "causes" in your family? How could "the man of the house" be more active as a leader in this area?

3. As a man, describe any regular spiritual exercises in which you engage (prayer, Bible reading, etc.). What, if any, improvements would you like to make in this area?

4. As a man, do you sometimes feel close to "burnout"? If so, how could improving your spiritual life help?

5. What male figures do you admire, perhaps to the extent that you might make them your "mentors"?

Notes

164

1. R. Kent Hughes, *Disciplines of Grace* (Wheaton, Ill.: Crossway Books, 1993), p. 187.
2. Joseph M. Stowell, "The Making of a Man," *Moody* (May 1992): 4.
3. Stu Weber, *Tender Warrior* (Portland Oreg.: Multnomah Press, 1993), pp. 213-214.
4. R. Kent Hughes, *Disciplines of a Godly Man* (Wheaton, Ill.: Crossway Books, 1991), pp. 17-18, adapted.
5. Hughes, *Disciplines of Grace*, p. 19.
6. Richard Exley, *The Making of a Man* (Tulsa, Okla.: Honor Books, 1994), p. 166, adapted.
7. Hughes, *Disciplines of a Godly Man*, pp. 76-77, adapted.
8. Ibid., p. 81.

The Ultimate Intimacy

If you would like an enriched and fulfilling sexual relationship with your wife, pray with her.

Now that I have your attention, let me explain.

If you want to discover the ultimate depth of intimacy with your wife, pray with her. If you want to resolve conflicts with your wife, pray with her. If you would like to begin to reveal yourself more to her, and to be less hesitant about engaging her in meaningful and fulfilling conversation, pray with her. If you would each like to feel more like allies and less like adversaries, pray for and with one another.

Possibly the most neglected area of Christian marriages today is praying together. Many couples pray *for* each other, but too few pray together. They don't realize what they are missing. Prayer is an integral part of being spiritually intimate.

What Is Spiritual Intimacy?

There are six dimensions of intimacy in a marriage: emotional, social, intellectual, physical, spiritual and recreational. We often define intimacy only in terms of the physical relationship. Men especially tend to put physical intimacy at the top of their marital priority lists. Women, however, tend to put emotional and spiritual intimacy higher on their lists.

What is spiritual intimacy? It is sharing and allowing the other person to glimpse into who you are spiritually. Spiritual intimacy is at times sharing your beliefs, at other times your doubts and sometimes even your unbelief. It is sharing your progress and your defeats, your times of triumph and your times of dismay.

Spiritual intimacy is also caring for each other spiritually.

I know couples who worship regularly together, but do not experience spiritual intimacy. I know couples who read Scripture regularly together, but have no spiritual intimacy. I know couples who pray and share together sporadically, but they lack spiritual intimacy. I even know some couples who don't pray and share, yet they do have spiritual intimacy.

What is the difference? The difference is attitude. Spiritual intimacy between partners in a marriage is a mutual, heartfelt desire to be close to God together, and to jointly submit to His direction for their lives.

Spiritual intimacy is the willingness to seek His guidance together, to allow the teaching of His Word to penetrate your everyday lives. It is a willingness to allow God to help you overcome your sense of discomfort in sharing spiritually, so you can learn to view your marriage together as a spiritual adventure.

Spiritual intimacy is the willingness to enthrone Jesus Christ as Lord of your lives and to look to Him for direction in your decisions, such as which house to buy, where to go on vacation, or which school is best for your children. As spiritual intimacy develops, He directs both of you in unity. He changes your hearts to be in agreement rather than speaking through just one of you.

PATTERNS OF SPIRITUAL INTIMACY

Many couples have discovered the benefits of growing together spiritually. John and Cindy Trent shared their growth throughout the years.

Over the years, my wife, Cindy, and I have taken specific passages that we have studied in God's Word and used them as a "personalized prayer guide" for each other. For example, take Psalm 15. That's a wonderful psalm where David lists ten traits that should be reflected in each Christian's life, then caps them off with a promise, "He who does these things will never be shaken."

With all the ups and downs of living in a stressful world, an "unshakable life" is currently something we both want to have! So we've taken the ten traits listed there and specifically prayed that they will be daily reflected in our loved one's life.

For example, "He who walks with integrity, works righteousness and speaks truth in his heart," becomes a personalized prayer for my wife: "Lord, may you keep Cindy walking in integrity; may she choose to do the right thing today, even in those times when it's difficult; and may your Word so fill her heart that her words to herself and to others echo your truth." Or, to apply another verse of Psalm 15 ("He swears to his own hurt and does not change"), she would pray for me, "Lord, may John be a man who always keeps his promises. Even if it's costly. Lord, may he always put commitment ahead of convenience."

Studying a passage together, then praying that God's truth will deeply reside in each other's life is a great way to build spiritual bonds!"[1]

Duffy and Maggie Robbins shared their experience.

When I asked Maggie how we had developed spiritual intimacy through our twenty-three years of marriage, her first response was to laugh. That worried me a bit.

We could both recall those early days of marriage when we would take time after the evening meal to read together through four chapters of the

167

Bible. And then, as we reminisced, she reminded me that I often ended those times with my head slumped over my plate, sound asleep as she read the last two chapters. I recall now that we decided to change our approach after a scary incident one night when I almost drowned in the gravy.

Then we both thought of those times when we pray together in bed—sharing our thoughts, frustrations, and hopes at the end of a busy day. While this is not a nightly habit, those times are precious indeed. Unfortunately, the problem again is drowsiness winning out over fervency.

Maggie explained our developing spiritual intimacy this way: "You have given me this wonderful, complete freedom to seek God and nurture a deeper relationship with him."

We have always thought of our marriage as a triangular relationship. We are at the two lower angles and God is at the top. The closer we grow to Christ, the more diminished is the distance between us. As we become one with Christ, so do we become one with each other.

I spend time with God early each morning before the house wakes up and the music starts. Maggie enjoys a leisurely devotional time after everyone has left for school and work. Neither of us insists that the other be involved in our devotional habits. But we freely share what we are learning in our individual pursuit of God.

I would say that our spiritual intimacy is not shaped by a shared mutual devotional pattern as a couple, but rather it is shaped by a shared mutual pursuit of intimacy with Christ.[2]

In more than 35 years of marriage, one of the discoveries Joyce and I have made is this: Developing our spiritual intimacy is the foundation for a lasting marriage. It is more than participating in spiritual activities together; it is an attitude or an atmosphere within the marriage relationship. It is the feeling of freedom that we can connect anytime and in any way about spiritual matters or issues. There is no walking on eggshells about sharing or raising questions. We live our lives in the confidence that we are connected spiritually.

In terms of the specifics of our spiritual growth together, we each maintain our own personal devotional lives. We daily pray with specific lists of prayer requests. We read from both the Old Testament and the New as well as other devotional material. Some days we read separate material, on other days it is the same.

Our time together consists of one of us praying aloud fairly regularly. Often during the day we bring prayer requests to the other's attention. Much of the time we read a devotional aloud, and have used several. Our church worship together is important to us, and frequently we discuss our responses to the music or message as we drive home.

Sharing the mutual grief of the life and death of our retarded son during the past 27 years brought us together spiritually. Through this we learned to share our hurts, concerns, frustrations and joys. What ministered to both of us during these times was worship. Not only did we worship at church, but also at home through worship music from a multitude of Christian artists and numerous music and inspirational videos. We have found that our personal and corporate walk with the Lord must be as much a priority and commitment as our wedding vows.

THE POWER OF COUPLE PRAYER

Praying for each other is the first step toward spiritual intimacy in a marriage, and an important one. Scripture calls us to do this.

> Pray for each other so that you may be healed. The earnest prayer of a righteous man has great power and wonderful results (Jas. 5:16, *TLB*).

Praying for another person by yourself is a safe practice because it involves no intimacy. That extra dimension occurs only when you tell the other person you are praying for him or her, or ask how you can best do so. Some partners have lived for years never knowing the other spouse was praying for them. What a support it is to know that you are thought of so highly that someone else is praying for you.

Patrick Morley, in his excellent book *Two Part Harmony*, discusses the benefits of praying for each other:

> Nothing our spouse can do for us can touch us so deeply as faithfully praying for us day after day, long after the normal person would have moved on to something new.
>
> Praying for our mate is another way of saying "I love you." It is an expression of loyalty to our partner.
>
> When we pray for each other we draw on the power of God to bring healing to our partner and lead him or her to wholeness. We say by our prayers that we are committed to bless and be a blessing to our mate.
>
> When we pray for each other our Father in heaven hears our prayers and, in accordance with His will, He answers them. Our prayers help unlock the rich treasures of God's kingdom for our spouse.
>
> When we pray for each other the attitude of our own heart becomes softer and more forgiving toward our mate. It is impossible to earnestly pray for someone and be filled with hatred for them at the same time. If we will start to pray, even if angry, the Lord will give us peace. As you pray for your partner you will find yourself letting go of your animosities, your reservations, your pettiness, and your insistence upon having your own way.
>
> When we pray for each other we deepen our love for our partner. To pray for our mate is to open us up to our mate. The more we pray, the more receptive we become to him/her. We begin

to see more of Christ in their lives. We begin to accept their weaknesses without so much condemnation. We begin to see that we are not as smart, wise, and spiritual as we may have thought.

When we pray for each other we deepen our partner's love for us. Through a spiritual operation our loving and gracious Father sews our hearts more closely together. Our heart is bonded to our partner when we know he/she is bringing petitions for us before the throne of God's grace.[3]

TOWARD REMOVING THE BARRIERS

Why don't couples pray together more? Some couples have simply never given it much thought. The idea never crossed their minds. Many others have said they didn't know any other couples who did. They had no role models or encouragement to do so. Others have given the common excuse that they don't have time. Pressures, work, children, interruptions—you name it, the excuses pile up.

Is there really any couple who could not carve out two minutes a day to pray together? Surely they could, even if it is while driving in the car, or going into the bathroom and locking the door and praying. Creative flexibility overcomes the struggle of time. We have discovered some of the external reasons for not praying, but there are also internal reasons.

Many couples believe they can't pray together because they lack closeness or intimacy. They believe that if their intimacy improved, praying together would become a possibility. They have it backward. It is not easy, but praying together actually creates warmth and closeness.

Praying together can also convict marriage partners about issues that need attention. You don't wait until everything is fine with the marriage and then pray. You pray to help it improve. If communication is difficult and strained, prayer may be the first step toward growth! Waiting until communication is perfect is like a Christian counselor trying to help a counselee get well without God, then later focusing on the spiritual dimension. It works just the opposite. The spiritual help must come first—and so must prayer together for a couple.

The fear of being transparent is a major issue. How do you know that what is shared will be taken seriously, won't be used against you or won't be seen as weakness? Let's face it—there is the risk of rejection within the very fiber of a marriage relationship. And we are all weak in some way.

Some couples are concerned because of their differences in spiritual maturity. Each, however, can learn to respect where the other person is, and pray in a way that both are comfortable.[4]

Differences in personality are often a factor. I've heard men say, "My wife is just much more articulate than I am. I sound like a child compared to her." Prayer is not a time to compare; it is a time to praise God for your individuality and uniqueness in personality. This uniqueness will manifest itself in your prayers just as it does in other areas of your life.

Partners who tend to condemn others during ordinary conversation usually do likewise when praying. Left-brained, analytical people reflect this tendency in their prayers, just as feelings-oriented people reflect a wealth of emotions when they pray. Extroverts formulate their prayers as they talk, whereas introverts want to formulate their prayers in advance. The prayers of articulate people usually flow smoothly Those for whom words don't come easily find it necessary to pause.

It may at first be awkward or even uncomfortable to pray together. Every phase of a marriage relationship that requires the finesse of coming together about something really worthwhile takes time to cultivate.

Many couples who learn to pray together begin with a very brief time of silent prayer. This enables them to safely experience their unique gender and personality differences. Most men prefer to put things on the back burner and think about them for a while. Thus, silent prayer may be less threatening to a man at first, but if he has the opportunity to reflect silently on what he wants to pray about, he will usually become more open to praying aloud. Some men prefer reflecting for a while first, then writing a prayer. Nothing is wrong with this. It takes time, courage and practice to develop a mutually beneficial prayer life, but it is worth the effort.

An exceptional book, *Praying with the One You Love* by Art Hunt (Questar Publishers) was released in the spring of 1996. If you would like a resource to help develop a prayer life together, this is the one!

THE BEAUTY AND THE BENEFITS

The benefits of praying together are numerous.

When a man and woman marry, they no longer think and act as single people. It is no longer "I," but "we." All of life is then lived in interdependence with another person. Everything you do affects this significant person. You're a team of two, and when both of you participate, you function better.

When you confront problems and crises in your life (and you will), a tremendous source of comfort and support comes from knowing another person will pray for you and with you. When you are struggling financially, or with problems at work, when you have tough decisions to make, or a medical crisis to face, sharing the burden with your spouse lightens the load .

173

Couples need to pray together for the health and security of their marriages. Marriage is a high-risk adventure. Your wedding vows will be attacked from all sides. Praying together will make your marriage stronger and help to protect you from the temptations that seek to destroy your marriage.

Scripture promises assure the effectiveness of prayer for married couples. Jesus said:

> Again, I tell you that if two of you on earth agree about anything you ask for, it will be done for you by my Father in heaven. For where two or three come together in my name, there am I with them (Matt. 18:19,20).

I believe we can't achieve our full potential together in marriage unless we pray together.

Couples who use prayer lists and see the results of answered prayer will be encouraged as they see how God works in their lives.

When couples pray together, disagreements and conflicts are reduced and resolved in the marriage. If you could see your spouse as a child of God, valuable and precious in His sight, someone He sent His Son to die for, wouldn't that have an effect on how you prayed for him or her?

In the book *If Two Shall Agree* by Carey Moore and Pamela Roswell Moore, Carey puts it plainly:

> To place Christ at the center of our homes means, of course, to tell Him, "You are God," not just at prayer time but all day long. I cannot be careless or insensitive in what I say to Pam and then pray with her. Nor can either of us treat anyone else rudely or engage in gossip and criticism or allow conceit and pride to rule our relations with others, and expect God to hear our prayers at the end of the day.
>
> Praying together involves the family finances, how we spend our time, what we do for entertainment, the thoughts we dwell upon when we are apart. I cannot be dishonest or profligate or stingy in money matters and then pray with my wife for His blessing on our economic life. Nor can we be cavalier with the way we spend money on clothes or a vacation or a new car, and then pray for the poor. I cannot harbor jealousy or hatred or lust or self-conceit in my thoughts, nor can Pam, and then expect God to hear us as we pray. When we come into His presence God searches our hearts. "Surely you desire truth in the inner parts" (Psalm 51:6).[5]

Sharing Each Other's Pilgrimage

A great way for you as a couple to encourage spiritual intimacy is to share the history of your spiritual lives. Many know where their spouses are currently in their spiritual walks, but very little of how they came to those places.

Use the following questions to discover more about your partner's faith:

1. What did your parents believe about God, Jesus, church, prayer and the Bible?
2. What was your definition of being spiritually alive?
3. Which parent did you see as being spiritually alive?
4. What specifically did each teach you directly and indirectly about spiritual matters?
5. Where did you first learn about God? about Jesus? about the Holy Spirit? at what age?
6. What was your best experience in church as a child? As a teen?
7. What was your worst experience in church as a child? As a teen?
8. Describe your conversion experience. When? Who was involved? Where?
9. If possible, describe your baptism. What did it mean to you?
10. Which Sunday School teacher influenced you the most? In what way?
11. Which minister influenced you the most? In what way?
12. What questions did you have as a child/teen about your faith? Who gave you answers?
13. Were you affected spiritually by an experience at a camp or other special meeting?
14. Did you read the Bible as a teen?
15. Did you memorize Scripture as a child or teen? Do you remember any now?
16. As a child, if you could have asked God any questions, what would they have been?
17. As a teen, if you could have asked God any questions, what would they have been?
18. If you could ask God any questions now, what would they be?
19. What would have helped you to grow more spiritually when you were growing up?

20. Did anyone disappoint you spiritually as a child? If so, how has that affected you as an adult?
21. When you went through difficult times as a child or teen, how did that affect your faith?
22. What has been the greatest spiritual experience of your life?

The Effect of Prayer on Marriages
We have talked a lot about spiritual intimacy and praying specifically, but does it really work? What effect does it have on a marriage? How does spiritual intimacy help you handle the crises and struggles of life and marriage?

The following statements are what a number of men said in response to the questions, *Describe the effect this has had on any other areas of your marriage,* and, *What effect has your spiritual relationship had on handling problems or crises in your marriage?*

Getting off each other's backs and concentrating on our own walks with God allows us to communicate more freely, and opens up the relationship for love.

We submit to Christ, so our family doesn't become a battleground of wills about how to solve problems.

As a couple, we share spiritual intimacy by praying together as a family at night. We pray for one another in the mornings (we try to do it often, but sometimes fall away from this good habit) by asking one another, "What can I pray about for you today?" Also we share in spiritual experiences together, i.e., being of Catholic faith, we participated in a couples weekend, which is a retreat-type weekend in which an encounter with Christ occurs (for each person in a different way), retreats, family camp at Forest Home each year, conferences, share individual experiences and insights that have brought about spiritual growth. Occasionally, we will share verses or readings that brought personal spiritual meaning. These all have brought us closer in our spiritual intimacy in our marriage. And though we have marital problems in other areas, our spiritual intimacy is growing. Because we desire as individuals to grow spiritually, we will endeavor to grow in our spiritual intimacy as a couple.

This spiritual intimacy growth helps us better accept one another. Though it hasn't cleared up certain problem areas, it has helped us cope with each other in those areas. Our spiritual intimacy has not increased our intimacy elsewhere (i.e., sex, conversation, etc.).

We have been drawn closer together in every way. It is difficult to separate love feelings, communication and sex as they are so intertwined, but I do feel that our communication has improved as a result of praying together, and that improves love feelings and sex.

177

Commitment to Christ meant I must deal with issues and not ignore or run from problems. I would tell my wife I had a problem or struggle and that I needed her to understand where I was coming from. I came to learn the health and growth of my wife was essential to a healthy relationship and achievement of my goals.

We pray together whenever we can. We don't pray every night before we go to bed or whatever, but if something is happening or she says something, I take her hand and we pray. We go to church. We have just purchased the *Couples Devotional Bible* and we own *Quiet Times for Couples* and we're anxiously awaiting Dennis Rainey's couples' devotional, *Moments Together for Couples*, which is going to be very practical (for my wife as well). But we don't really use those that often. We'll hit them on dates or once in a while and that kind of thing. We do worship together. We talk a lot. If something's going on, we spend most of our time talking it out. I'm a very emotional person; I need to talk about my emotions and figure out how those things are. We listen to Christian music almost exclusively. A lot of the music we end up talking about, and talking about other issues related to it and it kind of spins out from there. We're involved in a community group, as our church calls it, which is a small group Bible study where we deal with marriage and family issues as well as spiritual issues. So we're there and we're held accountable in that group. It's not all rosy.

178

Without a relationship with God I don't see how we would have made it through some rough times! Before we got married, I believed very strongly that my future wife knew God also. This was key to me, because when the impasses came, I knew that the same Spirit that was at work in me was at work in her. If I would respond positively to God and she would also, I knew we would make it. Many times the only thing that I could do to keep from self-destruction or blasting her away was to pray. I would either get away by myself or invite her to join me as I led us in prayer. I believe the focus on God and the mutual faith have pulled us to Him and to each other. It is fair to say, I don't know where I would be without God!

It has given us a freedom to talk and share. To look at biblical principles as well as reflect on our biblical responsibilities for the relationship.

We pray when we have problems, which cuts

down on arguing and we remind each other of the need to be mutually submissive. We respect each other's need for space and to talk with God before entering a disagreement that can potentially become heated.

The more we pray together, the closer we feel to God and each other. In addition we have become better at communicating our feelings in light of God's will. It is the most instrumental thing we've done to help us deal with issues, problems and crises. The more time we spend developing the spiritual aspect of our relationship, the more the other areas of our marriage (i.e., emotional, intellectual, social, sexual, etc., thrive and flourish).

The impact of our spiritual intimacy on our marriage has been quite profound. We have found that we argue much less often, and our temperaments have both been brought dramatically under the lordship of Christ over the past several years. We noticed that our children began to treat each other better. While they benefit from the anointing of the Holy Spirit upon our lives, they also benefit by having a home where they feel that their parents get along as well. We have established a new commitment to serve in outside ministries when both of us can serve side-by-side. For example, we both participate in the worship team for our church, we both lead the social committee, and we are a partnership in leading a home discipleship group. We find great satisfaction in watching God move mightily in each other. Our communication has improved dramatically. We share at a more intimate level than at any time in our marriage. My wife is able to share with me without the previous feeling of inadequacy, and I am more attentive to her needs. The most significant improvement has been the discovery that our physical intimacy is intricately bound to our spiritual intimacy. I had never understood this concept until I experienced it, and it is still a profound mystery. The Scriptures describe the coming together as one flesh, and I never quite understood the extent to which two people truly become one. There is something marvelous that happens at the spiritual level during worship when we intertwine our own spirits with the Holy Spirit. My wife and I have found that our most intimate physical encounters have followed our most intimate spiritual worship. When I found myself irresistibly drawn to her during and after worship together, I initially felt guilty for having such strong physical desires. I had thought that the two experiences must be mutually exclusive, as though the spiritual had nothing to do with our physical relationship. After we realized that God was Himself uniting us even more intensely during our times with Him, we found a wonderful freedom to experience a physical intimacy together after worship. Rather than exclude the Lord from our intimacy, He was actually teaching us how to be more loving, attentive, energetic, and serving with each other.

These men have made it work, and have shared the results. I have met many of these men. I know some quite well.

Men want adventure and challenge in their lives. What greater challenge can there be than to fully develop their potential by confronting resistance and then growing?

Spiritual growth is the last and ultimate frontier. These men's statements bear eloquent testimony that this frontier can be conquered.

REFLECTING ON THIS CHAPTER

1. Do you and your spouse find it difficult to pray together? If so, what steps could you take to realize increased intimacy in this area? (Example: Start out

by just reading a passage of Scripture together.)

2. Which of the six levels of intimacy mentioned in this chapter—emotional, social, intellectual, physical, spiritual and recreational—come most naturally for you? Which areas would you like to develop further?

3. Why does praying together increase the level of honesty and integrity between a couple?

4. Select several of the 22 questions in this chapter and discuss them as time permits.

5. *Action item:* Find out if there are resources in your area for a "Marriage Encounter" or other marriage seminar, and make plans to attend.

Notes

1. Les and Leslie Parrott, *Becoming Soul Mates* (Grand Rapids: Zondervan Publishing Co., 1995), p. 67.
2. Ibid., p. 59.
3. Patrick Morley, *Two Part Harmony* (Nashville: Thomas Nelson Publishing, 1994), pp. 10-11.
4. Carey Moore and Pamela Rosewell Moore, *If Two Shall Agree* (Grand Rapids: Chosen Books, 1992), pp. 30-42, adapted.
5. Ibid., p. 111.

A
CONVERSATION
ABOUT
THE FUTURE
WITH SOMEONE
YOU KNOW
AND LOVE

"God, I'd like to talk to You again."

"I'm here."

"I know You are. I have learned. There is nowhere that You are not. At least my theology is a bit clearer. You certainly gave me enough information about men....Or I should say the men did. It is a bit overwhelming. I guess my question now is, *Where do I go from here?*"

"Tell Me more about your confusion."

"Well, for instance, I understand more about the reasons men are *who they are* and why they are *the way they are*—their struggles, their fears, the tensions that exist between them and women. I understand what they need from women. But

I still need more insight about where to go from here."

"One of man's greatest struggles is between himself and woman. Years ago a man said about women, 'You can't live with them and you can't live without them.' That statement is true and it is not true. It is true that men cannot live without them. Both are My creation, created for each other. But it is *not* true that men cannot live *with* them. It can be done. It is not only being done, but it is also being done in harmony.

"Living together in harmony is a learning process. It is no different than growing in the Christian life. It takes time and effort. Remember the man who said, 'I need my wife to understand the fact that I do not want to die with it all inside'? Men need to share, not to bury the treasures I have placed within them. And women need to help men reach their goals!

"That was a profound insight on his part. But the completeness or restoration of men is not dependent on women. Women cannot heal the wounds of men, nor can men heal the wounds of women. Only I can give the healing and completeness they are searching for in their lives."

"I guess I have just a few unanswered questions. It is not that I haven't learned anything...I just want to be clear so my future is clear. I do not want my future to be determined by my past. I want to move forward in hope."

"Perhaps I can answer your questions without your asking them. I already know what your concerns are."

(Silence.)

"I guess You would know. All right. I'd like, uhh...I need to hear what You are going to say."

"I want you to remember that you and all humankind from the Tibetan peasant to the Bushman, the Estonian laborer to the American Congressman were all created to *serve* Me. Everyone is My workmanship—no one else's but Mine, created in My Son to do good works. Humanity is My work of art. Remember that you are the pinnacle of My creation. Do you understand that you were created in Christ Jesus? Anyone in Christ Jesus is a new creation. You have been made alive!

"In Christ you are being made totally new. Although Adam's sin programmed you for failure, your identity in Jesus is being redeemed and restored. You are being re-created and rebuilt into that which was stolen from you at the beginning of mankind by Adam.[1]

"I took your sin-dead lives and made you alive in Christ. I did this on My own with no help from anyone else. I did this to have You for Myself and to shower grace and kindness on you in Jesus. Saving you was My idea from start to finish. I created all of you to join Me in the work I am doing.[2]

"And I want all of you to do good works to *reflect Me,* to show your love for my Son and to follow Him.[3]

"My true disciples produce bountiful harvests. This brings great glory to Me.

"Whatever they do should be done to bring glory to Me.

"Are you called to preach? Then preach as though God Himself were speaking through you. Are you called to help others? Do it with all your strength and energy, so God will be glorified through Jesus Christ—to Him be glory and power forever and ever. Amen.[4]

"I did not call mankind to live for success or power. That distortion was created by the world. You have been called to be *My faithful* servant. The most important trait about a servant is that he does just what his master tells him to do.[5] Faithfulness will lead to success, but I will determine what success is.

"I want you to have a new attitude about work. This has been a constant struggle since the Fall. Whatever work a man or woman does is sacred. Work is designed to reflect Me. Your workplace is your mission field. I instructed Paul to tell the world this when he wrote, 'Whatever you do in word or deed, do it *all* in the name of Jesus. And whatever you do or say, let it be as a representative of the Lord Jesus, and come with Him into the presence of God the Father to give Him your thanks.'"[6]

"What can we as men do?"

"Surrender, but with new direction."

"Surrender? With new direction? Please explain."

"Mankind has been surrendering to the enemy's temptations for years. Surrender indicates that the battle is over after the determined outcome. When a man or woman surrenders to Me, however, surrender is made *in advance* of the battle and the surrender *determines* the outcome. Any person who surrenders fully to Jesus experiences victory—My victory. When you surrender to Me, remember, My power is greater than that of the enemy.[7]

"When men and women surrender to Jesus, they find He is the One who can help them face life—not just part of life, but *all* of it. Including the pain of the past. Jesus changes people. He deepens and strengthens their relationships. He equips and empowers people to face their stresses, troubles and pain.

"When men and women surrender to Jesus, I am able to do My healing work in their lives through the work of the Spirit.

"This may appear to you to be contrary to the world's point of view."

"Yes it does."

"Well, it is. The world says that you must control others to gain control. My way says that you get control by giving it up...to Me. Victory requires surrender to Me.

"Refusing to surrender to Jesus leaves you captive to unimaginable temptations. Surrendering to Jesus sets you free to resist temptation and gives you power to confront the struggles of life.

"What is the last message I have for you? It has already been said. It was written many years ago. It will always be true. Hear it. Accept it. Digest it. Live with it. Let it change your life.

"I showed how much I loved you by sending My only Son into this wicked world to bring to you eternal life through His death.[8]

"If you believe that Jesus is the Christ—that He is God's Son and Your Savior—then you are a child of Mine. And all who love Me love the rest of My children, too. In fact, I can tell how much you love Me by how much you love My children, your brothers and sisters in the Lord. Loving Me means doing what I tell you to do. It really isn't that hard at all; for every child of Mine can obey Me, defeating sin and evil pleasure by trusting Christ to help.[9]

"And you can be sure of this, that I will listen to you whenever you ask Me for anything in line with My will. And if you really know I am listening when you talk to Me and make your requests, then you can be sure that I will answer you.[10]

"So now, since you have been made right in My sight by faith in My promises, you can have real peace with Me because of what Jesus Christ your Lord has done for you.[11]

"So there is now no condemnation awaiting those who belong to Christ Jesus.[12]

"For My Holy Spirit speaks to you deep in your hearts, and tells you that you really are God's children. And since you are My children, you will share My treasures—for all I give to My Son Jesus is now yours, too. But if you are to share His glory, you must also share His suffering.[13]

"You are My workmanship, created in My Son for good works, which I prepared before you were ever created.[14] And as many men and women who receive My son, they have the right to become My children. If anyone is in My Son Jesus, he or she is a new creation. The old things will have passed away and all will become new.[15] You are a brand new kind of life that consists of continually learning more and more of what is right, and yielding constantly to be more and more like Christ who created this new life within you."[16]

187

REFLECTING ON THIS CHAPTER

1. This chapter envisions the questioner from chapter 2 asking a final question. Do *you* have other questions about men and male/female relationships that haven't been dealt with in this book?

2. What do you remember from this book about the "struggles, fears and tensions" that are typical of men?

3. What specific female traits do you think may have given rise to the cliché, "Women! You can't live with them and you can't live without them"?

4. What specific male traits might make it equally valid for women to say this about men?

5. The author says that men and women can't heal each other. What are the dangers for relationships when this is attempted?

Notes

1. Neva Cayle and Zane Anderson, *Living by Chance or Choice* (Minneapolis: Bethany House Publishers, 1995), p. 49, adapted.
2. Ephesians 2:8-10, paraphrased.
3. See John 15:8.
4. See 1 Peter 4:11.
5. See 1 Corinthians 4:2.
6. Colossians 3:17, paraphrased.
7. Gordon Dalbey, *Fight Like a Man* (Wheaton, Ill.: Tyndale Publishers, 1995), p. 7, adapted.
8. See 1 John 4:9.
9. See 1 John 5:1-4.
10. See 1 John 5:14,15.
11. See Romans 5:1.
12. See Romans 8:1.
13. See Romans 8:16,17.
14. See Ephesians 2:10.
15. See 2 Corinthians 5:17.
16. See Colossians 3:10.

DISCUSSION
LEADER'S
GUIDE

This book can be used as an informative tool not only to help
men understand themselves, but also to bridge the wide gap
of misunderstanding that exists between husbands and wives
about men. Careful study of this book will provide hope for
men who live in bondage to emotional isolation and fear. It is
intended to equip women to become facilitators for change.
Most importantly, *What Men Want* was written to help both
men and women discover God's magnificent design within
their differences and to perpetuate unity in Christ Jesus.

The optimum-sized discussion group is 10 to 15 people. A
smaller group may make continuity a problem when too few
members attend. A larger group will require strong leadership skills to create a sense of belonging and meaningful participation for each person.

If you are leading a group that already meets regularly,
such as a Sunday School class or weekly home group, decide
how many weeks to spend on the series. Be sure to plan for
any holidays that may occur during your scheduled meetings.

Use creativity. This book's 12 chapters will fit a regular 13-

week quarter, or they can be paired to provide additional weeks for personal sharing. You might even want to invite a guest speaker for one or two of the sessions.

The first session would provide a perfect time for an open forum to create a sense of unity before you begin the series. A time for introduction followed by nonthreatening questions is often helpful for building close ties within the group. Consider one or more of the following questions:

1. On a scale of 1 to 10, 10 being "brilliant," how would you rate your "what men want" IQ?
2. If you are a man, describe the perfect woman as you believe God designed her to be. If you are a woman, describe the perfect man as you believe God designed him to be.
3. In what ways do you believe God is asking you to stretch as you consider His ideal for your gender?
4. Why do you think God made men and women so different?
5. If you could ask God one question about the opposite sex, what would it be?

Such questions will create a sense of identity among the class members and help them to discover their similarities.

Many individual questions may arise that will significantly contribute to the group's understanding of the subject. Group members should be encouraged to maintain lists of their questions. Suggest that they be submitted anonymously and combine them together to obviate repetition. If you decide to have either a counselor or minister as your guest speaker, allow the speaker to address the questions. Many questions may be answered by the time the series reaches its conclusion. It is, therefore, a good idea to wait until your last session to discuss them.

Enlist a coleader to assist with calling class members to remind them of meeting dates, times and places. Your coleader can also make arrangements for refreshments and child care.

People will have a greater appreciation for their books if

they are responsible for paying for them. They will also be more apt to finish the course if they have invested in their own materials.

Be sure to have several extra Bibles available. *The Living Bible* would be helpful for people who have little or no Bible background.

Be aware of basic principles of group dynamics, such as:

1. Arrange seating in a semicircle with the leader included rather than standing in front. This setting invites participation.

2. Create a discussion-friendly atmosphere. The following tips are helpful for guiding discussions:

    a. Receive statements from group members without judgmentalism, even if you disagree with them. If they are clearly unbiblical or unfair, you can ask questions that clarify the issue; but outright rejection of comments will stifle open participation.

    b. If a question or comment deviates from the subject, either suggest that it be dealt with at another time or ask the group if they want to pursue the new issue now.

    c. If one person monopolizes the discussion, direct a few questions specifically to someone else. Or, tactfully interrupt the dominator by saying, "Excuse me, that's a good thought, and I wonder what the rest of us think about that." Talk with the person privately and enlist that person's help in drawing others into the discussion.

    d. Make it easy and comfortable for everyone to share or ask questions, but don't insist that anyone do so. Reluctant participants can warm to the idea of sharing by being asked to read a passage from the book. Pair a shy person with someone else for a discussion apart from the main group, and ask reluctant participants to write down a conclusion to be shared with the larger group.

e. If someone asks you a question and you don't know the answer, admit it and move on. If the question calls for insight from personal experience, invite others to comment on it. If it requires special knowledge, offer to look for an answer in the library or from a counselor or minister, and report your findings later.

3. Unless the group leader is a therapist or other professional trained in counseling, guard against trying to do group therapy. This doesn't mean that poignant moments won't come up or unhappy problems won't be shared, but the group is for sharing, not treating or fixing. The leader should be open and honest about wanting to grow with the group instead of coming across as an authority about the subject.

4. Start and stop on time, according to the schedule agreed upon before the series begins.

5. During each session, lead group members in discussing the questions and exercises at the end of each chapter, unless you sense that some of them might be too sensitive to be appropriately discussed in your particular group. If you have more than 8 or 10 class members, consider dividing into small groups, then invite each group to share one or two insights with the larger group.

6. Pray regularly for the sessions and the participants. God will honor your willingness to guide people toward more fruitful relationships.